THE SPIRIT OF CARNIVAL

THE SPIRIT OF CARNIVAL

Magical Realism and the Grotesque

David K. Danow

THE UNIVERSITY PRESS OF KENTUCKY

Publication of this volume was made possible in part
by a grant from the National Endowment for the Humanities.

Copyright © 1995 by The University Press of Kentucky
Paperback edition 2004

The University Press of Kentucky
Scholarly publisher for the Commonwealth,
serving Bellarmine University, Berea College, Centre
College of Kentucky, Eastern Kentucky University,
The Filson Historical Society, Georgetown College,
Kentucky Historical Society, Kentucky State University,
Morehead State University, Murray State University,
Northern Kentucky University, Transylvania University,
University of Kentucky, University of Louisville,
and Western Kentucky University.
All rights reserved.

Editorial and Sales Offices: The University Press of Kentucky
663 South Limestone Street, Lexington, Kentucky 40508-4008
www.kentuckypress.com

"Prishchepa's Vengeance" by Isaac Babel is reprinted from
The Collected Stories of Isaac Babel, © 1955
by S.G. Phillips, Inc., by permission of the publishers.

The Library of Congress has cataloged the hardcover edition as follows:
Danow, David K. (David Keevin), 1944–
   The spirit of carnival : magical realism and the grotesque / David K.
Danow
          p.   cm.
   Includes bibliographical references and index.
   ISBN 0-8131-1905-7 (alk. paper)
   1. Carnival in literature. 2. Magic in literature. 3. Grotesque in
Literature. 4. Fiction—20th century—History and criticism. I. Title
PN3352.C37D36   1995
809'.93353—dc20   94-42828

Paper ISBN 0-8131-9107-6

This book is printed on acid-free recycled paper meeting
the requirements of the American National Standard
for Permanence in Paper for Printed Library Materials.

Manufactured in the United States of America.

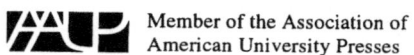   Member of the Association of
American University Presses

CONTENTS

1 / LITERARY MANIFESTATIONS   1
2 / THE CARNIVALESQUE-GROTESQUE   33
3 / MAGICAL REALISM   65
4 / GROTESQUE REALISM   103
5 / ARCHETYPAL ASPECTS   137
Notes   155
Works Cited   175
Index   181

For my Parents
whose Spirit remains
vital and alive

1 / LITERARY MANIFESTATIONS

> *The sensitive ear will always catch
> even the most distant echoes of a
> carnival sense of the world.*
> —Mikhail Bakhtin [1984:107]

From one important perspective that draws upon the positive attributes of carnival, it may be justly argued that this book is appropriately titled. There is indeed a life-affirming and life-enhancing "spirit" that pertains to carnival in its varied and numerous manifestations. But from an equally significant although principally negative standpoint, the present study might also have borne an opposite designation that likely would not be perceived or interpreted as innocuous. For the spirit hovering over the spectacle of carnival shares the stage with a lurking, less than benevolent, even demonic twin, which, in a sometimes flirtatious manner that can have disastrous results, will smile upon and favor death rather than life. So I might have chosen a title that also takes into account the "anti-spirit" of carnival. But titles, needless to say, need not take account of everything, and books likewise need not dwell so squarely and so prominently upon the jaundiced side of a common, perhaps universal, human preoccupation in the arts and in life.

Still, this study will afford no comparable indulgence in subsequent discussion of the concept of carnival. Suffice it to say at the start that both the positive and negative poles of experience are inextricably connected, as the common metaphor drawing upon polarity implicitly suggests, and will be treated accordingly in the following exploration. A positive, life-affording potential, in other words, will be shown to coexist in uneasy alliance with a corresponding affinity for its fugitive negative realization. Further, in accord with my intention to make of this work a literary investigation, my arguments, examples, and suppositions are derived fundamentally from primary sources in the form of contemporary literary narrative.

I must nonetheless note that those same rich and diverse sources are framed in these opening pages by theoretical views belonging to Mikhail Bakhtin, the Russian literary theorist and philosopher of dialogue. The closing arguments of the book are likewise framed by the thought of the Swiss psychologist Carl Jung, whose theory of the archetype plays a summative role in my findings here. Within those twin "frames," the subject of carnival, in its multifarious *literary manifestations,* is explored through a range of brief citation and extended reference that embraces seemingly insignificant incidents as well as fully developed drama belonging exclusively to the realm of fiction. Finally, in this opening series of caveats, the term "carnival" itself must be acknowledged as not entirely appropriate to the topic of this book, since my subject is the "carnivalesque"—a rich and complex designation that will, however, require book-length clarification.

The twin concepts of "carnival" and the "carnivalesque" represent two distinct but interrelated considerations. Carnival originates in ancient times. Its precise origin remains a matter of scholarly debate. As Sir James Frazer holds in his encyclopedic work *The Golden Bough* (1890), the diverse ceremonies of death and rebirth that characterize carnival, with its mock conflagrations and attendant symbolic resurrections, "bear the stamp of a dateless antiquity" (1963:367).[1] In its most general sense, carnival celebrates the body, the senses, and the unofficial, uncanonized relations among human beings that nonetheless exist, as Bakhtin affirms in his acclaimed study of medieval folk culture, *Rabelais and His World* (1965), alongside the official, openly recognized forms of human intercourse. My purpose in this work, broadly stated, is to explore how these two sets of relations are manifested in the intentionally perpetuated discourse that is twentieth-century literature.

What are our perceived differences between carnival and the carnivalesque? The first refers to an established period in time when certain cultures engage in a spirited celebration of a world in travesty, where the commonly held values of a given cultural milieu are reversed, where new "heads of state" are elected to "govern" the ungovernable, and where the generally accepted rules of polite behavior are overruled in favor of the temporarily reigning spirit of Carnival. When a similar spirit permeates a work of literature, we suggest that it partakes of or promotes the Carnivalesque. That is, it supports the unsupportable, assails the unassailable, at times regards the supernatural as natural, takes fiction as truth, and makes the extraordinary or "magical" as viable a possibility as the ordinary or "real," so that no true distinction is perceived or acknowledged between the two.

For present purposes, "carnival" is understood to refer generically to concrete cultural manifestations that occur periodically in numerous related forms in North and South America, Europe, and the Caribbean. Carnival is defined by folk culture temporarily subordinating to itself certain "hidden," embedded features of the official culture that may include the particular use of language and dress (including the profoundly important mask), as well as the introduction of a fool, madman, or clown to serve as a necessarily short-lived "regent." In addition, the people arrange for themselves, as simultaneous participants and spectators, a spectacle (of theater, music, and dance), in which they may (un)ceremoniously partake. This generalized activity we distinguish from the "carnivalesque," which, as the operative term here, designates the general application of a certain carnival "spirit" (whose sense and meaning will be discussed throughout these chapters) to the world of literature, which responds in multifarious but related ways to an attitude that is both social and cultural, mythological and archetypal. In effect, the carnivalesque provides a mirror of carnival; it is carnival reflected and refracted through the multi-perspectival prism of verbal art.

Hence, in this usage, the "carnivalesque" denotes a diverse "carnivalized attitude," or "spirit," reflected in a myriad of equally varied yet necessarily related manifestations in world literature. It designates "the transposition of carnival into the language of literature," to which Bakhtin refers appropriately but cumbersomely as "the carnivalization of literature" (1984:122).

Victor Terras speaks of "a universal human impulse toward carnival as a revolt against and reversal of fixed values" (1991:519). In broad terms, my intention is to examine that "revolt" and "reversal" of what we implicitly understand as fixed, traditional, or conventional values, as rendered in modern novelistic treatments. To that end, the present study represents a necessarily delimited treatise that concentrates on two literatures: the twentieth-century novel of Latin America and the literature engendered by the European experience of the Second World War. My purpose is to demonstrate a certain commonality between these two apparently incommensurate sources that derives from a particular attitude toward the world and the world of literature, which attitude, I will argue, is embraced by the carnivalesque.

This study, therefore, does not examine instances of actual carnival, its concrete manifestation at a specific time and place. It focuses instead upon the carnivalesque: carnival's reflection in literature, a mode and perspective that at once produce transformations, reversals, and inversions of fate and fortune that reveal in turn a resultant, necessarily dualistic view of the world. Likewise, my chosen concentration is upon selected works of literature that reflect the Second World War experience rather than focus upon the war itself and the experience it generated in reality. I make this important distinction at the outset in order to remain free from all possible constraints to speak about a particular carnival as concrete cultural event or about the actual Holocaust, a telling case in point, as historical fact. My topic is, then, narrative, a mode of human communication and an artistic form for reflecting one world (the actual) in another (which is fictional).[2]

Within the general framework of the carnivalesque, the aim of this study is to explore its bright, life-affirming, "magical" side as well as its dark, death-embracing, horrific aspect. The former is broadly exemplified by Latin American "magical realist" works; the latter is most profoundly revealed in novels engendered by the sufferings inflicted upon millions during the Second World War. The most terrible event in the history of the world produced an equally extraordinary literature to reflect that awful period. Since this study is determined by concerns that are literary and philosophical rather than social and historical, attention here will concentrate on the literature produced by that experience—on the "literary fact" (in the Formalist critic Jurij Tynjanov's felicitous phrase), as opposed to historical event. Further, in our practice, the term "Holocaust" pertains generally to accounts of suffering experienced during the Second World War. This broad perspective on that vexed expression will allow, for instance, for the torturous experience of a young dark-haired, dark-eyed boy traipsing through the unspecified countryside of Eastern Europe during the war years, as documented in Jerzy Kosinski's *The Painted Bird* (1965), to figure prominently within our subsequent discussion. At that stage, the inverse of the magical aspect will be seen, in effect, to emerge as the horrific side of life, as unrelenting terror monumentally experienced.

In discussing Dostoevsky's *The Idiot,* Bakhtin observes that "Myshkin [the novel's saintly hero] is in carnival *paradise,* Nastasya Filippovna [beautiful, tortured, and damned] is in carnival *hell*" (1984:173). In this study, I will expand upon Bakhtin's insightful but limited distinction between carnival heaven and carnival hell by making extended reference to the two profoundly important strains in twentieth-century world literature, previously noted: the magical realism of Latin America that responds to the mythological and cosmological beliefs that still animate the world of indigenous tribes living in the southern half of the Western hemisphere, and the works of disparate writers scattered throughout the world who, up to the very present, still respond to the horrors experienced in Europe a full half-century ago. In Arthur Koestler's *Arrival and Departure* (1943), the argument is put forth that "since the Renaissance, the red tissue paper of our scientific reasoning has obtained greater perfection than the blue of our intuition and ethical beliefs" (1968:210). In discussing the literature of Latin America, the blue, in effect, will be given its due. At the same time my discussion of Holocaust literature, whose historical source had been determined by a specious and cruel "scientific reasoning," will be refracted through a "tissue" lens that has been forever turned blood red.

In a sense, the two seemingly disparate literatures selected for joint analysis here represent a certain continuum in world literature. Both appear fantastic, straining credibility. Yet one presents essentially the bright side of human experience: the wide range of man's potential combined with a corresponding, even greater potentiality that exists in the extended world of nature. The other literary manifestation reveals the darkest side of human capacity, what would have been unimaginable had it not actually happened. Latin American readers of magical realist works recognize their world and their experience within that world. They may acknowledge as well that what is documented is not only remarkable but also, paradoxically, ordinary; that what is depicted, however imaginatively refracted in artistic fashion, nonetheless represents the everyday experience of Latin America—what Gárcia Márquez refers to as "an immediate reality that came to be more fantastic than the vast universe of . . . imagination" (1971:44).[3] By contrast, the reader of Holocaust literature is bound to be aware of the horror as extraordinary. Yet both literatures spring from what is, or had been, mundane experience.[4] (It is not for nothing that Hannah Arendt speaks of the banality of evil.) Dictators and revolution are common in Latin America, as its literature makes eminently clear; the forced transports in cattle cars of human beings to the death camps were equally a part of the European experience during the war.

Still, that seemingly neat division of "separate realities," reflected in two apparently distinct literatures, does not preclude the equally distinct possibility that their respective characteristic features may at times coincide. In Gárcia Márquez' quintessential work of magical realism, *One Hundred Years of Solitude* (1967), the fantastic is presented as commonplace among the "peddlers of everyday reality" (1971:43). One chapter begins thus: "It rained for four years, eleven months, and two days." That matter-of-fact statement is shortly followed by the remark that "the worst part was the rain was affecting everything and the driest of machines would have flowers popping out among their gears if they were not oiled every three days" (1971:291-92). So, alongside the "commonplace fantastic," there also exist practical concerns. Further, this carnivalized reality does not preclude an attendant grim potential from emerging as well in all its darkest manifestations. Hence, on an individual plane, one character proclaims: "The only effective thing . . . is violence" (100); while another asserts: "for people like us [shooting is] a natural death" (154).[5] In such equations is rooted an affinity for violence that is not only personal but cultural, a collective "truth" that can easily explode—as in the joyous celebration that is quickly transformed into its deadly counterpart, a "bloody carnival" (186) devouring its players.

> Innocent of the tragedy that threatened it, the town poured into the main square in a noisy explosion of merriment. The carnival had reached its highest level of madness. . . . Suddenly, during the paroxysm of the celebration someone broke the delicate balance. . . . The rifle shots drowned out the splendor of the fireworks and the cries of terror drowned out the music and joy turned into panic. . . . and there were many dead and wounded lying on the square: nine clowns, four Columbines, seventeen playing-card kings, one devil, three minstrels, two peers of France, and three Japanese empresses. [191-92]

"The delicate balance," a hallmark expression in the present context, is broken, affording a striking example in which the bright carnivalesque is seen to elide with the dark grotesque.

Even more telling is a later occurrence in the same novel, when striking workers are summoned to gather at the town square to receive redress for their grievances. The result is again mass murder, as the innocent are cut down by the strange "hallucination" (283) of machine gun fire. According to a now sadly familiar pattern, "the nightmare trip of the train loaded with corpses traveling toward the sea" (for instant burial and elimination of evidence) is followed by denials (that seem to follow all such atrocities) that the terrible event ever occurred in the first place. " 'There haven't been any dead here.' . . . 'There weren't any dead.' . . . He could find no trace of the massacre. . . .There were no dead. . . . 'Nothing has happened . . . nothing has ever happened, and nothing ever will happen. This is a happy town' " (285-87). Reminiscent of the literature of the Holocaust, the grim reality depicted in these passages of the premier work of magical realism is the same, only the metaphors differ: "Those who had put them in the [railroad] car had had time to pile them up in the same way in which they transported bunches of bananas. . . . Through the wooden slats as they went through sleeping towns he saw the man corpses, woman corpses, child corpses who would be thrown into the sea like rejected bananas" (284). Here the analogy is between human beings and bananas, elsewhere it is between people and cattle. The awful point remains the same.

Yet the respective emphases of the two literary forms differ. What magical realism portrays is ultimately positive, affording a hopeful vision of life in which what might be termed fantastic is designed to appear plausible and real. In

Holocaust literature, the fantastic emerges as horrific rather than "magic." Where one form illustrates the endless potential for life, the other (largely determined by historical fact) reveals a powerful tendency toward death, as the fugitive success of the innocent survivor appears a greater oddity than the rewarded efforts of the determined killer. Broadly stated, the profound difference between the two may be conceived as situated on a continuum whose poles reflect the classic opposition between eros and thanatos, between the force for life and the drive toward death that occupies, at one and the same time, the human soul.

How that opposition is realized in literature is an implicit concern of this book, posed in a series of interrelated questions: How can we understand the stunning and engaging magical realist texts of contemporary Latin America in light of highly contrastive European representations of equally compelling twentieth-century realities? Are these two seemingly oddly matched forms related in their varied literary manifestations? Are they diametrically opposed? Or, do we find certain points of tangency? The answers to these and like concerns will afford new understandings not only of these two pertinent and significant modern literary forms but of the sources that generate them.

As noted, it may appear that one literary form is situated at one extreme of the continuum of human potential and the other at the opposite end, as seeming polar opposites or as two sides of a kind of Janus face of human experience. One laughs, the other cries. One gazes in joy and wonder, the other stares fixed in horror. One appreciates the vast potential for surprise in the world, relative to man's place within it; the other is aghast at a like potential for extreme cruelty and brutality.

Literary Manifestations

But what if these two seeming ends of a continuum were shown to meet? What if this "continuum" were molded in the form of a circle, with each of its two polarities then joined? Or, as Nietzsche expresses this dilemma in *The Birth of Tragedy* (1872): "When the inquirer, having pushed to the circumference, realizes how logic in that place curls about itself and bites its own tail, he is struck with a new kind of perception: a tragic perception, which requires, to make it tolerable, the remedy of art" (1956:95). For present purposes, what is needed (not to denigrate the role of art) is the remedy of a new model—one that is newly conceived. In the subsequent course of discussion, this book takes up the challenge posed by just such problems. At this early stage, suffice it simply to acknowledge the power of metaphor to sway—perhaps even determine—our thinking. Were one to persist in taking the notion of an "absolute" continuum as a model exclusively, one would necessarily have to insist on the myriad differences between the two literary forms chosen for discussion here to the virtual exclusion of their occasional significant similarities.

The point is made by Jung that "between all opposites there obtains so close a bond that no position can be established or even thought of without its corresponding negation, so [that] '*les extrêmes se touchent.*' " He goes on to say, paradoxically: "True opposites are never incommensurables; if they were they could never unite" (1960:206-7). On the intuitional plane, which in part accounts for this book and which Jung clearly valued, the Swiss psychologist notes "the archetype's affinity with its own opposite," remarking as well the image of the "tail-eating serpent" (213). While the present study makes no claim for its subject being identified purely as an archetype (a point to which I will return), Jung's insistence upon the affinity one pole or extreme has for its opposite helps to make the case for our own "tail-eating" model (an image that, curiously, as we have seen, Nietzsche also draws upon in referring to that kind of logic that "curls about itself and bites its own tail").

As another (figurative) feature of this mode of thinking, the appropriateness of the Janus face as model is likewise supported by a range of disparate literary works. In the magical realist tradition, we read in Isabel Allende's *Eva Luna* (1987) that a woman gives birth to a child "characterized by a fused body with two heads. . . . The great curiosity was that one head was white by race, and the other black" (1989:103). Typically, in this tradition, it is left to readers to make of that "fact" what they will, but within the present exploratory context, the event may turn out to be not so much a "great curiosity" as part of a clearly established pattern that is, in essence, dualistic in nature.

That duality extends to the other literary tradition to be explored here, as instanced when the Janus face model endures a peculiar split in Yoram Kaniuk's *Adam Resurrected* (1972), in which the engaging mad protagonist continually startles those around him. "How can this man cry in pain with one eye and with his other laugh like a wise guy?" (1972:75), asks a fellow inmate of the mental institution where both reside. Laughter, as a response to horror and a means for survival, is (as we shall see) deeply rooted in a literary tradition preoccupied with both terror and surmounting its effects. In more general terms, the Janus face is indeed an appropriate model for our purposes, since, as seems evident: "All the images of carnival are dualistic; they unite within themselves both poles of change and crisis: birth and death . . . blessing and curse . . . praise and abuse, youth and old age, top and bottom, face and backside, stupidity and wisdom" (Bakhtin 1984:126).

As an extended theme (rather than a peculiar isolated incident), *The Campaign* (1990) by Carlos Fuentes begins with, and is based on, a related carnivalesque reversal: a well-born white child is kidnapped and exchanged for a prostitute's black baby. "He moved quickly: he put the black child next to the white one in the cradle. He contemplated them both for a few seconds. Thanks to him, they were fraternal twins in fortune. But only for a moment. He took the white baby and wrapped him in the rags of the poor child; then he swaddled the black one in the gown of high lineage" (1992:16). The passage succinctly illustrates a basic principle of the carnivalesque: a reversal in fortune achieved by an individual of low position removed to one that is high, making the transition, in effect, "from the kennel to the throne" (Kaniuk 1972:247)—in contrast to the situation in tragedy, where the protagonist suffers a fall from grace—but which new situation is destined to last "but only for a moment." In Fuentes' work, that moment is even further truncated, since a fire occurs almost immediately after the switch, leaving the black baby burned to death. The intent of the hero of the novel, himself "an agent of the blindest, most involuntarily comic justice" (1992:59)—that is, an agent of the carnival spirit of (in)justice—is clearly, although childishly and idealistically, motivated: "What he'd dreamed was now a reality. A black child condemned to violence, hunger and discrimination would sleep from now on in the soft bed of the nobility. Another child, white, destined for idleness and elegance, had lost all his privileges in a flash and would now be brought up amid the violence, hunger, and discrimination suffered by the blacks" (21-22).

True to the carnivalesque spirit of reversal and inversion in which this novel is grounded, the hero's "dream" may be perceived as both just in abstract terms (Why should one child be assured a better life than another, especially on the specious and cruel basis of the color of its skin?) and unjust in its particular (lawless) application. This dualistic feature, coupled with the strange, strained turn of events represented by the subsequent conflagration, affords an immediate, second carnivalesque reversal: the stolen child (white), made as good as dead for his parents, remains, nonetheless, alive; the switched child (black), offered up to a life of riches, on the other hand, dies instantly. The carnivalized result of the hero's confused, confounded efforts to right—in oblique miniature— a widespread social wrong results in greater injustice. ("He had only substituted one injustice for another." 43)[6] In addition, illustrating the slippage typical of the carnivalesque reversal, the initial high idealism that motivated the act may be just as accurately expressed in the cynical language of the gutter: "Now this son of an expensive whore will live the life of the son of a cheap whore" (34). In the philosophical terms that carnival also rightly elicits, and drawing in part upon the present illustrative instance, we see that the carnival spirit inspires the transformation of absence into presence: what cannot be, for a moment, *is*; what is least likely emerges as temporarily established fact. In a world of "infinite possibility," the carnivalesque inspires the realization of the least expected eventuality, as the unimaginable is conceived and created out of a bewitched idealism that wants to see change, no matter the cost.

In this political novel, and in the world at large, that change is frequently effected—and the cost made high—by revolution. In Fuentes' argument, however, "all modern revolution does is create a new elite. Why? The old elite was more elegant and practiced in the very thing the new elite is going to do: mete out injustice" (127). According to this line of thought, "all modern revolution" (although in the context of this novel we are talking about events that are nearly two centuries past) achieves is a carnivalesque substitution on the same order as that accomplished by the switching, on a microcosmic scale, of a white baby for a black one. The tiny "political act" upon which the novel hinges, in other words, mirrors the greater political event of revolution, where the end result is the same: instead of one force meting out injustice, another is put in its place to do exactly the same thing. To that end, as this work and the contemporary Latin American novel in general acknowledge, insurrection and (civil) war are the most time-honored means. When the unlikely hero of *The Campaign* makes his first kill, and in order to "kill from then on with a clear conscience," he attempts an act of propitiation. "I tried to transpose the face of my victory on the battlefield onto [the dead man]. . . . The mask of glory passed over without any difficulty from my face to his, covering it with a rictus of horror and violence. . . . I fled the place as soon as I felt that both faces, mine and that of my victim, were changing once again. It was no longer glory. It wasn't even violence. Once the masks of war were gone, the face that united us was that of death" (107-8).

As in Dostoevsky's *Crime and Punishment,* the crucial lesson learned is that the one who takes the life of another human being kills off a part of himself in the process. The potential for violence and death represents the dark side of the carnivalesque. In the passage just cited, the possibility for transformation is again realized; the human face once more is shown to bear a dual aspect. But the series of transformations documented here are not only from the "face of victory" to a "face of death"; also noted are the significant shifts from a face that is human to a mask that is demonic, indicating, in these twin shifts, not only the swiftness by which death may become the eternal substitute for life but also the speed by which what is human becomes dehumanized through the taking of a life. For the hero, the dead soldier becomes "my propitiatory victim, my memorable dead man," who will allow him, *now,* to kill "without thinking twice about it" (107). But in that "now," that new, unchangeable, and fearful contemporaneity, the face of the hero has been forever altered from that of an innocent to that of one who has killed—and, in the subsequent course of the novel, he is perceived as having changed as a result of having acquired that dire experience. Returning to the notion of a continuum, or, better, to our Janus face model of human experience, we recognize that the hero has just shifted, in that one *simple* deed, from the one side that is bright and smiling to the other, which is diminished and sad.

In a very dissimilar modern work, a like Janus face is suggested by the repeated reference in Alexander Solzhenitsyn's *Cancer Ward* (1968) to "the place where ninety-nine weep but one laughs" (1969:531). A commonplace of Western criticism asserts that Solzhenitsyn's novel represents in microcosm, within the cancer ward, the macrocosm of Soviet society. That commonplace may be profitably extended to suggest that the phrase just cited, pointed in its indictment of the Gulag Archipelago concentration camp system and poignant in its human implications, incorporates a view that again acknowledges the dark side of the carnivalesque attitude in modern literature: namely, that within this greatly proliferated tradition, there is a steady alternation, as well as a simultaneous manifestation, of writings animated not only by carnivalesque laughter but also by tears. Hence, there should be no quarrel with Gárcia Márquez' (earlier cited) fugitive reference to a "bloody carnival" atmosphere, a seeming oxymoron but nonetheless a felicitous phrase that speaks potential volumes.

One such volume is the 1928 novel *The Street* by Israel Rabon. In this little known work (which deserves greater recognition), there is a passage that looks back as it were to the popular culture of the marketplace that absorbs Bakhtin in his study of the medieval carnival atmosphere, emanating, as he puts it, from "the free winds blowing from the marketplace" (1968:275). The winds blowing in Rabon's novel, however, howl in anticipation of a literature that will be born only after the Second World War in response to atrocities that had not yet made their fully developed appearance on the world stage. This novel anticipates that development, particularly in a scene that ostensibly takes place during the Russian Civil War.

> The next morning we were led to the marketplace again. Our hands were tied, and we were forced to undress and to lie down half naked on the ground. Our shoulders were smeared with ground meat mixed with human excrement and animal dung. Each man lay half a meter or so away from the other. Then more than a hundred pigs were driven into our midst. The pigs, squealing wildly, tore at our naked shoulders. Not far from us, thousands of people looked on, delighted by the atrocious spectacle. Many of the prisoners had parts of their shoulders gnawed away by the pigs. [1990:103]

Reminiscent, on the one hand, of Kuznetsov's *Babi Yar* (and of passages borrowed from that work and incorporated into D.M. Thomas' *The White Hotel*), several aspects of this account nonetheless bear unmistakable Rabelaisian features: the marketplace as setting, the presence of copious amounts of food as well as excrement, the overwhelming sense of a feast (indulged in by a hundred pigs no less), the theatrical aspect, as "carnival becomes a theater of cruelty" (Lachmann

1987:7). After all, the passage represents an instance of "popular culture" witnessed and enjoyed, we are told, by thousands of people. Yet, in stark contrast to the preponderant literature of the past (left largely untouched by the possible influence of de Sade), that "atrocious spectacle," in its wholesale gruesome aspect, stands as a quintessential instance of twentieth-century writing, one that also provides an accurate prefiguration of far worse yet to come.[7]

In a singular reversal of roles (between the human and animal world), Isabel Allende's fine political novel *Of Love and Shadows* (1984) offers a related image in which the swine, this time, is brutalized as a direct result of *its* being politicized.

> At the construction site of the monument to the Saviors of the Nation an enormous pig was released, costumed in cockades, a Presidential sash, a dress uniform cape, and a general's cap. The beast ran squealing through the throng, who spit on it, kicked it, and hurled insults at it before the eyes of irate soldiers who used every trick to intercept it in order to rescue the trampled sacred emblems; finally, amid screams, sticks, and howling sirens, they shot the beast. Nothing remained but the enormous humiliated carcass lying in a pool of black blood on which floated the insignia, the kepi, and the tyrant's cape. [1988:274-75]

Again, the cruel side of the carnivalesque is depicted in all its rich, dark potentiality—which includes the blatant irony of enacting in travesty the frequent like fate of the generic swinish despot, dispatched, in the end, by a barrage of bullets emanating from the guns of precisely those who are supposed to protect him.

In a like dark context, there is a relatively innocuous but related instance of a modern carnivalized passage in Juan

Literary Manifestations 19

Rulfo's *Pedro Paramo* (1959), a stunning "novel of Mexico" (as the work is subtitled). In this tale, the character whose name gives title to the novel has just lost the love of his roguish life, a woman who would not countenance him and who died, seemingly, through pure self-will, again seemingly, at least in part, to spite him.

> At daybreak the village was awakened by the ringing of the bells. . . . At noon they were still ringing, and at nightfall. They rang day and night, day and night, louder and louder and louder. The people of the village had to shout in order to hear what they were saying.
> "What's happened?" they asked.
> After three days everybody was deaf. It was impossible to talk with that clamor filling the air. And the bells rang and rang. . . .
> The endless ringing began to draw people in from other places. They came in . . . almost as if on a pilgrimage. . . . A circus arrived from somewhere, with a merry-go-round and a ferris wheel. And then the musicians. They were only spectators at first, but soon they were playing in the bandstand in the plaza. Little by little the occasion turned into a fiesta. . . .
> The ringing stopped at last, but not the fiesta. There was no way to explain to the crowd that the bells rang for the dead, no way to make them go home. On the contrary, more and more arrived. [1969:114-15]

In this passage, in which only the feelings of the hero are brutalized, there are also the familiar topoi of the marketplace (the plaza) as setting, the sense of a feast (fiesta), of music and celebration, the drawing of an immense crowd, resulting in general hilarity and excitement—all of which are again entirely inappropriate to the situation at hand. That inappropriateness, however, is also a kind of topos, a modern counterpart to what Bakhtin refers to as the "unofficial" culture of an earlier age. Thus impropriety, although seemingly unwitting, plays its part—in which, this time, the acknowledgment of death is transformed into a celebration of life. In essence, as will be shown, such transformations, reversals, or inversions typify the carnivalesque in their relentless shifting from life to death and back again.

The role of the marketplace or central square figures inherently as a principal feature of the carnivalesque. As such, that primary role inspires further consideration of a "poetics of the street" in acknowledgment of that place where virtually anything can, and often does, happen. The street is a real-life stage upon which the most unexpected drama may be enacted, including the drama of Carnival. On the individual plane, the street is where, potentially, one's fortune and destiny are ultimately played out. As part of the public domain, the street is also the stage for public demonstration. That is where—on the historical scale—governments topple and sometimes fall. In the wake of one such (fictional) uprising, where thousands take to the streets, we find this telling remark: "The crowd roared its approval so enthusiastically that it almost seemed like Carnival" (Allende 1989:134). Inevitably, a study of carnival and a like investigation of a poetics of the street are bound to converge.

In that convergence, as only a single, exemplary case in point, what might be explored is the notion that "established authority and truth are relative" (Bakhtin 1968:256). In this study, the critically related overarching question is, How is that relativity expressed in narrative? In partial response to this complex, multi-faceted question, we may say broadly at this stage that the carnivalesque attitude, among numerous other sources, serves as an implicit model for the making of a

Literary Manifestations

wide array of texts that explore in various ways precisely this problem of "relativity." Conversely, specific (psychological, sociological, linguistic) aspects of a work generated by such a model are bound to reflect that originating carnivalesque attitude: in a single telling phrase, in a work's basic governing structural principle, or in a vast array of carnivalized situations and events. Revealing encapsulations of the carnival spirit (within a work that may nonetheless be a veritable bastion of carnivalized activity) include such telling remarks as these:

> The world has bewitched me. [Fuentes 1992:64]
>
> The universe surrounding him had the smell of a festival about it. [Asturias 1982:101]
>
> We're all kind of demonized. [121]
>
> One thing there's no shortage of anywhere are whorehouses and churches. [Vargas Llosa 1988:435]
>
> That's what they have most of there. . . . Churches and funeral parlors. You can get dizzy from all the religions they've got. [481]
>
> It's guaranteed by three thousand years of popular wisdom. [Gárcia Márquez 1980:54]
>
> For [the townspeople] the supernatural was more believable than the natural. [Vargas Llosa 1985:99]

Analogous to such pithy pronouncements in its own terse relation to the carnivalesque, Mario Vargas Llosa's *Conversation in the Cathedral* (1969) allows for hardly a single carnivalesque image in the entire sweep of this political novel of six hundred pages. Yet, in direct contrast to such paucity, the basic structural pivot of the work is founded on a clear carnivalesque principle: the inextricable bonds that exist between government officialdom, high society, and the demimonde that affords the upper strata of people in power their principal source of entertainment.

On the other hand, Miguel Angel Asturias' novel *Mulata* (1963), reminiscent of the paintings of Hieronymus Bosch, is a veritable textbook of the carnivalesque. Replete with countless transformations and reversals of fortune (that are themselves frequently reversed once again), it depicts the intermixing of human affairs with those of demons and devils (but not with gods or goddesses), making for a pronounced, sustained blend of the natural and the supernatural; the presence of grotesque laughter at nearly every turn, coupled with the forces of darkness triumphing over the (essentially absent) forces of light; the seemingly never-ending introduction of devils, demons, and sorcerers; saints, priests, and (un)holy men; dwarfs, giants, and all manner of tricksters; wizards, witches, and spooks; and "a certain Mulata." In sum, the novel affords an astounding presentation of an overwhelmingly "different order or disorder of ideas" (1982:203), which makes of the book a virtual compendium of metonymically linked notions, united only by their increasingly outrageous, demonic points of view, which are governed by a principle of organization that can only have been derived from a carnivalized attitude toward the world and all its wonders.

The carnivalesque therefore represents not so much a single literary form as a complex *form of thought* "that had coalesced and survived for thousands of years among the broadest masses of European mankind" (Bakhtin 1984:123), a (perhaps primordial) way of thinking, or an archetypal pattern, whose distinctive imprint may be found in a vast multitude of literary works. Bakhtin insists upon "the deep philosophical character of carnival" (1968:252). The aim here is to explore the carnivalesque, carnival's profound reflection and varied manifestation in modern literature, where cultural values derived from "established authority" appear fluid in relation to a concept of "truth" that also remains in flux.

As a point of departure, let us turn to Bakhtin's assessment of the carnival attitude—what he terms "the general world outlook expressed in the popular-festive carnival forms" (244). His conclusions are derived from linked sources: his joint analyses of Rabelais' masterwork of sixteenth-century French literature, *Gargantua and Pantagruel,* and the attendant medieval culture that served to generate that work. Designed to capture the medieval carnival attitude, Bakhtin's model points up several prominent features: the clear absence of a serious tone, carnivalesque revelry marked by blatant openness and recognition of new forms of linguistic and cultural expression, "freedom and lack of ceremony . . . balanced by good humor," and "complete liberation from the seriousness of life" made distinctly evident within the "atmosphere of carnivalesque freedom and familiarity." Last, in this abbreviated summation, that same atmosphere elicits a "wish for death and the wish for life. . . . [a revival of] the ancient ambivalence of the death wish, which also sounds like a wish for renewal and rebirth: die, and live again" (245-49). So, in brief, says Bakhtin in the context of an earlier reality that could never have conceived the twentieth century. Now, in recognition of more recent, grim historical fact, that phrase might well be reversed: live, and die again. Survive at your own peril.

But all such relative issues—even those of life and death, and perhaps, especially those—are dependent, first of all, upon the dominant political and cultural attitudes of a given time and place. Our present concern is with the fluid relation between "established authority and truth." If, as the old maxim has it, truth is relative, we may inquire once more as to how that relativity is realized in literature. A second viable response is to draw upon a common figurative notion of dialogue by suggesting that the carnivalesque affords a certain "dialogic exchange" between the official and unofficial modes of cultural expression. In addition, we may borrow from Bakhtin his basic model of the Self and Other, conceived as dialogically engaged communicants seeking to understand one another. Through slight emendation, a renewed but still meaningful model emerges: the Official Self in dialogue with the Unofficial Other, where the two will inevitably exchange roles, borrow from one another in the course of their "discourse," allowing for certain acceptable (as well as unacceptable) reversals and transformations to take place that will ultimately yield a variety of "truths," distinguished by a single unifying feature: their basically peripheral and ephemeral nature. No truth, in other words, is ever *the* truth.

Further, within the same context of a "dialogized carnival" or "carnivalized dialogue," there clearly remains evident another greatly pertinent possibility: namely, that of a like figurative exchange within the carnivalesque between its bright, life-affirming quality and its dark, death-embracing aspect, between the beatific and the demonic, "spirit" and "anti-spirit." In effect, those designations once again encapsulate the main topic of this book, whose aim is to elaborate in various instances and on a variety of levels precisely such "dialogue," and to reveal its ultimate result. Part of the way in which that carnivalized dialogue proceeds is to remove all obstacles to its obstinate progress by obscuring the boundaries between seeming hard and fast oppositions—the official and unofficial, life and death—in an ongoing effort to merge these opposing forces into new configurations of truth and meaning. Yet these newly born forms will in turn bear the seeds, in true carnival fashion, of their own eventual dissolution. Not only is truth peripheral and ephemeral but so are the (phantom) borders that distinguish meaning. In carnival, in other words, boundaries do not exist.

As Bakhtin would agree, himself greatly preoccupied with the question of borders (among speech utterances, speech genres, and speakers as well), the carnivalesque is animated by a certain, perhaps periodic, human *need* to dissolve borders and to eliminate boundaries, so that there might be "an element of carnival play with death and the boundaries of life and death" (Bakhtin 1974:295). Hence, the carnivalesque is designed to allow one extreme to flow into another, to provide for one polarity (the official culture) to meet and intermingle with its opposite (unofficial culture), much as individuals engaged in dialogue exchange points of view that may on occasion converge or coalesce into a single perspective.

Just how prolific the carnivalesque spirit can be in its wanton destruction of established boundary is illustrated splendidly by Rulfo's *Pedro Paramo*. In this novel of dissolution, where distinctions among commonly delineated entities are consistently destroyed, a hallmark exchange takes place between the leading dissolute figure—the book's fearless (and, in that sense, heroic) anti-hero, Pedro Paramo, who is bent at all costs on imposing his will—and his man who is, mainly, his henchman.

> "It's a question of boundaries. He's putting up fences and he wants us to put up our part, to finish dividing."

"Don't worry about boundaries. There won't be any. Remember that . . . even if you don't understand it." [1969:35]

Not only will territory not be bounded, but much else as well in this remarkable novel will likewise resist (de)limitation. Thus commonly conceived boundaries are destroyed—beginning with those between the living and the dead.

"No. You're not crazy, Miguel. You're dead." [20]

"They've killed your father."
"And who killed you, Mother?" [22]

"You don't have to be afraid any more. They can't frighten you now. Just think about pleasant things, because we're going to be buried for a long time." [59][8]

As a further dimension of this carnivalesque erasure of common distinctions, people the hero does not know are summarily relegated to a category of non-being, since, for him, they "don't even exist" (63). On her wedding night, a young bride has her best friend substitute for her in her husband's bed, instituting the first in a series of exchanges and substitutions in which one living body will do as well (or nearly so) as another. (" 'A handful of flesh,' he called her. And when he embraced her he tried to change her body into that of. . . 'A woman who isn't of this world.' " 107) In this wondrous text, the boundaries are dissolved as well between mother and father ("I'm your father too, even though I'm your mother" 28); and between the "spiritual" and biological mother ("They told me in Heaven that they'd made a mistake. They said they'd given me the heart of a mother, but not a mother's womb" 58). The voices cf the dead ("voices worn out with use"), as well as "old laughter," mix with living sounds, producing a haunting echo effect. ("The village is full of echoes. Perhaps they got trapped in the hollows of the walls, or under the stones" 39.) This is so because "the village is full of spirits, a whole throng of wandering souls that died in sin" (51). One still hears the howling of the dogs in this haunted place, which is the world, even though "there aren't any dogs here any more" (40). Even the presumed unity of the self is dissolved into a curious blend of what we have referred to as the self and other.

> I saw a man cross the street.
> "You!" I called.
> "You!" he called back. In my own voice. [41]

Certain biological functions are likewise reduced to a lack of fundamental distinctions; hence, inhalation and exhalation, the air breathed in and out, becomes an indeterminate unity, or, in keeping with the spirit of the book, a nullity. ("There wasn't any air. I had to swallow the same air I breathed out, holding it back with my hands so it wouldn't escape. I could feel it coming and going, and each time it was less and less, until it got so thin it slipped through my fingers forever. Forever." 56) Likewise, the body's individual organs are collapsed into one another. ("Then she felt that her head was crushing into her stomach. She tried to separate them, to push her stomach aside, it was blinding her eyes and cutting off her breath, but her head pressed down and down, as if it were sinking into the darkness of the night." 114) Time itself resists definition; unbounded and unchanged, it remains precisely the same as it had been—before.

> "It's been a long time since you left me, Susana. The light was the same as it is now. Not so reddish, but just as weak and cold, because the sun was hidden by the

clouds. Everything's the same. It's even the same moment. I was here at the gate, watching the dawn. Watching you go away. Watching you climb the path to Heaven. And Heaven opened up, and light streamed out. You left the shadows of this world behind you. You vanished into Heaven's light." [116-17]

Lastly, in this lyrical prose narrative, filled with both spirit and gore, the great artificial distinction between poetry and prose—or, better, between what we term poetic and what we call prosaic—is also felicitously erased.

Essentially the same might be said of the works of the great Russian writer Isaac Babel, whose *Red Cavalry Tales* (1926), drawn from an entirely different context, find a common theme in revolution with Rulfo's novel and numerous others of the Latin American tradition, where revolution and political upheaval are characteristic (as we shall see) not only of magical realism but of its carnivalesque source as well. In mining that source, I cite in its entirety "Prishchepa," Babel's stunningly compacted miniature narrative, one of the single most powerful pages in world literature, included in his well known cycle of stories devoted to the Russian Civil War.

> I am on my way to Leszniow, where the Divisional Staff is quartered. My companion, as before, is Prishchepa, a young Cossack from the Kuban—a tireless ruffian who has been turned out of the Communist Party, a future rag and bone man, a carefree syphilitic, and a happy-go-lucky fraud. He wears a crimson Circassian coat of fine cloth, and a downy Caucasian hood is thrown back over his shoulders. On our journeys he has told me his story.
>
> A year ago Prishchepa ran away from the Whites. In revenge, these took his parents as hostages and put them to death. Their property was seized by the neighbors.

Literary Manifestations

When the Whites were driven out of the Kuban, Prishchepa returned to his native settlement.

It was early morning, daybreak. The peasants' slumber sighed in the acrid stuffiness. Prishchepa hired an official cart and went about the settlement collecting his phonographs, wooden kvass-jugs, and the towels his mother had embroidered. He went out into the street in a black felt cloak, a curved dagger at his belt. The cart plodded along behind. Prishchepa went from neighbor to neighbor, leaving behind him the trail of his blood-stained footprints. In the huts where he found gear that had belonged to his mother, a pipe that had been his father's, he left old women stabbed through and through, dogs hung above the wells, icons defiled with excrement. The inhabitants of the settlement watched his progress sullenly, smoking their pipes. The young Cossacks were scattered over the steppe keeping the score. And the score mounted up and up—and the settlement remained silent.

When he had made an end, Prishchepa went back to his despoiled home and arranged the furniture he had taken back in the places he remembered from childhood. Then he sent for vodka, and shutting himself up in the hut, he drank for two whole days and nights, singing, weeping, and hewing the furniture with his Circassian saber.

On the third night the settlement saw smoke rise from Prishchepa's hut. Torn, scorched, staggering, the Cossack led the cow out of the shed, put his revolver in its mouth and fired. The earth smoked beneath him. A blue ring of flame flew out of the chimney and melted away, while in the stall the young bull that had been left behind bellowed piteously. The fire shone as bright as Sunday. Then Prishchepa untied his horse, leaped into the saddle, threw a lock of his hair into the flames, and vanished. [1960:108-9]

In this utterly spare account, we find several prominent features representative of, and generated by, the carnivalesque. First, there is the sense of theater, of an extended spectacle replete with numerous spectators (saving their own hides at a healthy distance), as well as a single, principle performer working his will on any number of unwilling participants. The slaughter that takes place represents the primordial ritual of vengeance (traditionally frowned upon by official culture but a vital and viable activity in popular culture), accomplished on a grand scale. That kind of scale is emblematic of the carnivalesque and is matched in this miniature tale by eating and drinking with Rabelaisian abandon. Finally, there is the all-consuming presence of fire—designed to swallow the old in preparing the way for the new. As Bakhtin puts it (in his discussion of "popular-festive forms"): "The heart of the matter is the ambivalent combination of abuse and praise, of the wish for death and the wish for life, projected in the atmosphere of the festival of fire, that is, of burning and rebirth" (1968:248). In the "festival of fire" that concludes "Prishchepa," we find all of these ingredients in compact abundance. The "abuse" mentioned is explicit and extreme; the "praise" is implicit and is directed at both the hero's parents and a life that is gone forever. The ambivalent "wish for death and the wish for life" are clearly present in Prishchepa, who will take his revenge in order to go on living in the only way he knows: according to a code that demands vengeance.[9] But in this way, he also challenges an entire village to rise up against him and put a stop to the ritual by putting an end to him and his misery. Last, the "burning" within the story is also the burning that went on literally, somewhere in Russia, for four years (1918-1922), leaving the path finally cleared for the "rebirth" of a nation, whose subsequent demise the world has just recently witnessed.

Literary Manifestations

Implicit within my argument is the view that human beings are animated, in their art making, by a periodic predisposition toward the bright side of the carnivalesque, matched by a potentially far darker predilection for what we might term (with obvious and extended caveats) the grotesque. Bakhtin rightly combines (in recognition of their potential convergence) the two concepts in a single expression, the carnivalesque-grotesque. Further, the continuous communal effort on the part of the world's art makers is determined by historical factors as well as by others clearly belonging to prehistory. The following chapters are therefore designed to show that the expression "carnival forms" (realized as the carnivalesque) is essentially synonymous with "forms of thinking" and, moreover, that *carnival forms of thinking* are firmly embedded within the human psyche as primordial structures, or ancient modes of conceptualization, that find their frequent reflection in otherwise seemingly disparate literary forms.

Bakhtin writes: "The influence of carnival, in the broadest sense of this word, was great during all periods of literary development. However, this influence was in most cases hidden, indirect, and difficult to detect" (273). My purpose here is to search out and detect precisely that influence in two apparently unrelated contemporary literary modes and to show as well that this influence is both universal and archetypal.

2 / THE CARNIVALESQUE-GROTESQUE

*Through the window they saw a light
rain of tiny yellow flowers falling.
They fell on the town all through the night.*
—Gabriel Gárcia Márquez [1971:137]

*The university library was hit and burned;
for days afterward, in addition to the
steady rain of undifferentiated ash . . .
entire calcined pages of books fell from
the sky.*
—Louis Begley [1992:117]

In his study of Rabelais and medieval folk culture, Bakhtin argues that the "carnival-grotesque form" exercises a particular function that may be expressed from a series of related views: "to consecrate inventive freedom, to permit the combination of a variety of different elements and their rapprochement, to liberate from the prevailing point of view of the world, from conventions and established truths, from cliches, from all that is humdrum and universally accepted. This carnival spirit offers the chance to have a new outlook on the world, to realize the relative nature of all that exists, and to enter a completely new order of things" (1968:34). Yet that new outlook on the world, despite Bakhtin's pervasive optimistic spirit (with which he looks upon the positive potential inherent in dialogic engagement as well as carnivalesque "celebration"), will likely bring its share of bad along with the good. That is, no matter how the argument gets loaded ("consecrate," "liberate" vs. "cliche," "humdrum"), there is still the potential for something to go awry, or askew, in the common slippage from theory to practice. So the carnival attitude promises joyous renewal but may well deliver something less desirable as well.

In those works pervaded by a presumed "carnival spirit," in other words, there may also be evident a correspondingly sober perspective that likewise deserves attention because of inherent juxtapositions within a given work as well as for the message delivered. Bakhtin acknowledges this, in effect, when he says: "In world literature there are certain works in which the two aspects, seriousness and laughter, coexist and reflect each other, and are indeed whole aspects, not separate serious and comic images as in the usual modern drama" (122). We will see this confirmed in a single composite literary form, Latin American magical realism, which, while heralded for its cheerful presentation of the utterly unexpected, may reveal as well an uncompromising, grievous aspect that is equally a part of the reality it depicts. Further, the dark side of the carnivalesque will also be explored in the contrastive terms suggested earlier, encompassing the seemingly unrelated spheres of Latin American and Holocaust literatures, which largely define our comparative project here.

A distinction Bakhtin ostensibly makes between earlier literary forms will serve to distinguish between the contemporary modes under discussion. He differentiates the medi-

The Carnivalesque-Grotesque

eval and Renaissance grotesque from what he likewise describes in general terms as the Romantic grotesque. First, the term linking the two—the broad concept of the grotesque—may be seen to embrace within its vast domain a fundamental sense of exaggeration, hyperbolism, and excessiveness; an impulse toward "the breaking up of the established order," and a feeling of "immeasurable and exaggerated dimensions"—in sum, a reliance on excess as the measure of a new (but not yet accepted) standard. Moreover, in accord with Hugo, we may say that "the aesthetics of the grotesque are to a certain extent the aesthetics of the monstrous" (41-45). Yet, in our later consideration of certain texts (*The Painted Bird*, for instance), Hugo's cautious caveat ("to a certain extent") will appear superfluous, as the grotesque and the monstrous converge, becoming synonymous.

Part of what makes the term "monstrous" suitable in terms of twentieth-century literature may be derived from the following observation: "The grotesque image reflects a phenomenon in transformation, an as yet unfinished metamorphosis, of death and birth, growing and becoming" (24). But what if the twin concepts of "growing and becoming" are eliminated? What if the notion of "unfinished metamorphosis"—the idea, perhaps, of something aborted, left incomplete, in disarray, partially destroyed, not quite dead—emerges as *final* and triumphant? In response, we need think only of the literary (and filmic) images of the concentration camp victim, that horribly emaciated soul not quite alive, not yet dead. ("Wretched, nerve-racked hopeless sticks. . . . Beautiful grotesques." Kaniuk 1972:51) In contrast to this stark reality, Bakhtin argues: "All the episodes are ambivalent: destruction and uncrowning are related to birth and renewal. The death of the old is linked with regeneration; all the images are connected with the contradictory oneness of the dying and reborn world" (1968:217). But, again, what if there is no such ambivalence? What if "regeneration" appears distinctly absent, yielding no corresponding image of a "reborn world"? In that case, we are left in the firm, unrelenting grip of one extreme from among the two polarities delineated by the Russian theorist.

The first such polarity is typified by the medieval and Renaissance grotesque, whose most significant weapon is laughter, the source of a vital regenerative power. In this literary form, traditional worn-out values are vanquished; what is tired and effete is defeated; even death is conquered by the reiteration of new life, affirmed in the cycle that leads from death to rebirth: "The phenomenon in its becoming, in its movement from the negative to the positive pole. . . . the world passing through the phase of death on the way to birth" (411-12). In the eventual transformation of the medieval and Renaissance grotesque into the Romantic grotesque, the main result is the loss of the power of regeneration. Instead, a certain fear of the world and its hazards becomes the new message of uncertainty and insecurity.

As a needed antidote, fear must be subordinated to laughter (although "sometimes fear is laughter" Asturias 1982:167), what David Patterson treats as "metaphysical laughter," explaining: "When the word is exiled from its meaning, when the symbols of truth become signs of nothing, when the silence of the sky transformed into a cemetery is deafening—laughter remains the one avenue to life, the sole distinction between life and death" (1992:125). Curiously, a fine sense of what is meant by laughter in this context is provided by an unlikely source, Eli Wiesel's classic work of Holocaust literature, *The Gates of the Forest,* in which the twin manifestations of madness and laughter are treated poetically and philosophically. "Behind every tree and within every shred

The Carnivalesque-Grotesque

of cloud someone was laughing. It was not the laughter of one man but of a hundred, of seven times seven hundreds" (1967:17). True to the carnivalesque tradition, this depiction of laughter is collective at the core, belonging not to a single individual but to the world's inhabitants at large. It is rendered not in response to what is funny but in answer to what might otherwise (without its healing power) be frightening. Thus, Yoram Kaniuk's madman Adam instructs his fellow asylum inmates and concentration camp survivors in the collective spirit that Bakhtin acclaims in Rabelais: "There is just one outlet. Only one way to rescue yourself. To laugh. . . . If I had been unable to laugh there . . . I couldn't have taken it, I would have died from it, and the same goes for everybody, for all of you. Men and women, him and her, you and you. . . . You have to know how to laugh. There's no other way" (1972:184). Because, as Renate Lachmann points out: "Cosmic laughter dispels cosmic fear" (1987:13).

Laughter, in this tortured context, thus remains the last resort of the hunted, just as it belonged to the "folk" in the medieval period that is the subject and focus of Bakhtin's study. In fact, while the two contexts (the medieval and the modern) are clearly different, the two understandings (belonging to Bakhtin and Wiesel) are the same. When we read in Wiesel's work that a hunted-down figure "in the face of the soldiers and the stupefied dogs. . . burst suddenly into overwhelming laughter" (1967:60), that laughter can be traced to the folk tradition, revealing a popular stratagem for overcoming fear (and perhaps, in a moral sense, one's tormentors), documented as far back as Rabelais. But this stratagem is also depicted in the poignant terms of the present: "Once you conquer your fear everything looks different. I'm happy now that I've conquered my fear. All my life fear has tortured me shamefully, you understand, shamefully. Now I'm a free man"

(Appelfeld 1983:103). That not so small triumph, after all, is the goal "in those pyromaniacal years of dread" (Kaniuk 1972:232): freedom—but freedom, first of all, from fear.

How do we account for laughter's "longevity"? Why is laughter so powerful? In short, because within "the power of laughter [is contained] the power of life over death" (Patterson 1992:127). In Bakhtin's words, "Laughter has a deep philosophical meaning, it is one of the essential forms of the truth concerning the world as a whole. . . . Certain essential aspects of the world are accessible only to laughter" (1968:66). Examining the idea in its philosophical dimension as "an essential form of truth," as well as its being a vital source of the literary imagination, Patterson argues: "Metaphysical laughter takes the man beyond the confines of space and time, of fear and isolation; it has a ring of madness about it, of a mad struggle for possibility, without which there is no resurrection. . . . Laughter is the means by which madness turns back on itself" (1992:126-27). In such critical terms are revealed a certain inspiration for the making of literature. As Wiesel relates in *The Town Beyond the Wall*: "To laughter you can only oppose laughter." Through laughter you can "show destiny that you aren't afraid of it, that it's no stranger, that you can make fun of it, laugh in its face"—even if that face is the ugly mug of the executioner. Laughter allows you to "shed your illusions . . . fling off a dead weight, the weight of death" (Wiesel 1969:92). The fear of death is thus countered in the only way it can be: by the will "to go down laughing" (147).[1]

That courageous will, in the face of impending death, is documented in two of Wiesel's early novels. "He laughed . . . with neither joy nor cruelty, with the laugh of a man who has known total fear and is no longer afraid of anyone or anything" (1967:27). Such transformation, or liberation, we are bound to understand, is effected in the same freedom-seeking manner that Bakhtin explores in his study of a very different time. Yet the formula (or prescription) remains the same: one cures fear by laughter. But which "one"? In Wiesel's terrible world, it is the lonely, abandoned one who is mad—not having gone mad, but having *chosen* madness as his course;[2] as the only, necessarily paradoxical, resolution to a world gone mad, a "world that was insane" (Allende 1988:284). But that still leaves open the question, Who is the madman? Wiesel provides an answer (that also takes into account Allende's disturbing designation): "In times like these madmen are our only friends. They don't kill us in the name of beliefs or ideas. They're on our side and they get themselves killed" (1967:23). "They are the salt of the earth" (Kaniuk 1972:50), as one figure, herself quite mad, puts it in carnivalized terms. Problematic as it may sound, when one must choose from among three possible roles, that of victim, killer, or indifferent spectator, madness, as defined by Wiesel (and as we shall see), may well appear the only virtue.

Significantly, the main differences between the Renaissance Grotesque and the Romantic grotesque, as argued by Bakhtin, appear most distinctly in relation to terror. On the one hand, "the medieval and Renaissance folk culture was familiar with the element of terror only as represented by comic monsters, who were defeated by laughter. Terror was turned into something gay and comic." A commanding resource ever at hand, laughter, according to this vision, could always be called upon to defeat fear. On the other hand, "the world of Romantic grotesque is to a certain extent a terrifying world, alien to man. All that is ordinary, commonplace, belonging to everyday life, and recognized by all suddenly becomes meaningless, dubious and hostile. Our own world becomes an alien world" (1968:38-39). That image of an alien world—in whose unrelenting grip we find ourselves fearfully caught—characterized by terror, hostility, and the loss of meaning, is, in its most extreme expression, perhaps nowhere more forcefully formulated than in the literature of the Holocaust.

Of definitive importance to our developing thesis, then, what Bakhtin has to say about medieval and Renaissance grotesque, with its attendant regenerative laughter, bears greatly on Latin American magical realism. Similarly, what he has to say about Romantic grotesque relates closely to the literature of the Second World War. In these two contemporary literary forms, a related opposition exists between what can be generalized broadly (for the moment) as a celebration of life in all its varied manifestations and a grim and sombre acknowledgment of death as an equally colossal consideration.

In magical realism, death figures in the carnivalesque sense that Bakhtin perceives in popular-festive imagery; it allows for (re)birth and new life. There is a regenerative feature evident in its humor and consequent laughter, first of all, but also in the sheer proliferation of life forms documented in Latin American writings indigenous to the jungle and the sea, to both land and water. In the literature of the Holocaust, there is the repeated depiction of death without its carnivalesque, regenerative effect. "Death throes are" *not* "combined with birth in one indissoluble whole" (435). Where there is death, in this form, there is only death, with its accompanying terror devoid of any (life)saving grace. Yet, in our schema, that great negativity in the one literary form allows us to perceive it as the dark side, or back side (as Bakhtin might have it), of the other. Further, this view correlates with the tradition of the carnivalesque, in which there exists "the constant combination of falsehood and truth, of darkness and light, of anger and gentleness, of life and death"

(433), typifying a world view that is characterized by ambivalence and duality.

In a "dualistic world," where such ambivalent phrase itself may refer to the actual world, the literary world, or a carnivalesque depiction of the one (the actual) refracted through the prism of the other (literary), the conclusive sense of a duality that affords something greater than singularity is (in each case) ultimately achieved. That something, as expressed by Bakhtin, is "the fusion of the past and future in the single act of the death of the one and the birth of another." This vision, it may be argued, has its place in magical realism.[3] Yet the understanding of "grotesque" that adheres, for example, to the notion of a "grotesque historic world of becoming and renewal" (435-36) is surely not the grotesque of Holocaust literature, where there is no sense of "renewal." There, the past can (and must) be remembered, to paraphrase the famous saying of Santayana, in order to preclude its "rebirth" in the future.

Between Holocaust literature and the Romantic grotesque there exist certain parallels and similarities. Most notably, there is a governing concept of terror that supersedes the very possibility of regeneration and renewal. Yet to conflate the contemporary form with an expression that is anachronistic would at the least be inappropriate, even more so because the term "Romantic," with all its attendant trappings, runs counter to the essential quality, or spirit, of this singular literary form. However, in seeking a designation that, for our purposes, would be more expansive or inclusive than "Holocaust literature," which also bears considerable trappings of its own—as well as a profound emotional coloring—we will borrow from Bakhtin the concept of "grotesque realism."[4] As he puts it, "The essential principle of grotesque realism is degradation" (19); "debasement is [its] fundamental artistic principle" (370). Such formulations are absolutely essential and appropriate to our present concerns. "Grotesque realism" will therefore serve as our basic operative term, in accord with a process of substitution that allows us to proceed from Bakhtin's joint preoccupation with the gay carnivalesque and degrading grotesque to an exploration of contemporary magical realism juxtaposed to grotesque realism, in which the inverse of "magic" is recognized as horrific.

Given this inverted relation, it appears reasonable that we find arcing across both literary forms the interconnected themes of various authoritarian figures, whose soldiers, police, and sundry sadists, are empowered to torture and kill (in seeking out some ephemeral "truth") without accountability. This theme is treated in brilliantly sustained fashion in Gárcia Márquez' *The Autumn of the Patriarch* (1975), a quintessential magical realist work studded with wondrous event, astounding hyperbole, and all manner of excess typical of the form. Yet it also portrays, alongside the horrors of dictatorship, with its wanton cruelty perpetrated upon a helplessly enduring but patient people, the resilience of those who may know little but can be certain of one thing: that they are destined to outlast their "patriarch."

This novel affords a carnivalesque vision of dictatorship and despotism in which the central figure, the "patriarch" himself, father of his people (and of innumerable, unacknowledged bastard children)—in his insatiable longing for adulation, his driving need for power, and his repeatedly demonstrated ability to thwart the perceived and imagined efforts of all possible (and impossible) pretenders to the throne, his remarkable inability to see himself as the people perceive him (as an incomparable monster), his operating on sheer whimsy, his cruelty, viciousness, avarice, and plain meanness—resembles no one so much as that great Kremlin disciple of Machiavelli and the Devil, Josef Stalin.[5] Nonetheless, *The Autumn of the Patriarch* presents in brilliant, complex literary form an anatomy of Latin American dictatorship maintained by an elaborate military apparatus, coupled with a still more refined organization of government-sanctioned, institutionalized torture chambers.

Part of the complexity inherent in this novelistic account of a monstrous Caribbean tyrant derives from its being not only replete with magical realist detail but also by its being fully integrated at every turn with equally startling, horrific account. On the one hand, the despot changes at whim the time of day as well as the dates of national holidays, causes an eclipse of the sun by decree, placates the raging tides of a hurricane, reverses the course of a river, and has the light of the sun and the glow of the stars tinted red. At the same time he also orders countless executions and assassinations. Only learning to read and write (after a fashion) as a very old man, the great leader, "the one who gives the orders" (as he is called) is illiterate but has a terrible genius for murder. Yet that very "genius" cannot obscure the telling fact that "it was impossible to do away with such a quantity of life without leaving a trace of horror that would travel around the world" (1977:105). That assumption captures the singular essence of the book: namely, that this novel shares equally in the twin realms of the carnivalesque and the grotesque. While stunning attention is paid to magical realist detail, full of marvelous and exaggerated event, there is also a complementary sober attitude, drenched in irony, directed toward the corresponding horrific fact of a cruel despotism that permits a people's enslavement, mass persecution, and murder.

How are these two perspectives filtered through this single literary work? The answer is to be found in the unique prism of the carnivalesque, whose vision or "spirit" encompasses both the bright light of human potential and the accomplished evil present at times in man's treatment of man. In Gárcia Márquez' exemplary novel, this dualistic attitude is manifested in the carnivalization of time, sickness and death, the commonly accepted relations between the animal and human worlds, related associations between man's inner and outer worlds, and in further relations based on paradox, oxymoron, and exaggeration. Regarding the latter set of skewed possibilities, the reader is informed that "there were no secrets of state that were not in the public domain, there was no order that was carried out with complete certainty" (125). That does not mean, however, that orders were not issued with an absolute assurance that was "unmistakable and fearsome" to those informed of the general's implacable will. Thus, his quaking henchmen are told: "within a maximum of forty-eight hours you find him alive and bring him to me and if you find him dead bring him to me alive and if you don't find him bring him to me" (143). Paradoxical many times over, such "reasoning" is clearly the hallmark of a carnivalized world in which "there was always another truth behind the truth" (45), concealing or disguising, behind a mask (as it were) of eternal dissimulation, "the hazards of reality" (13) that ultimately prove overwhelming to both ruled and ruler alike.

The book's opening lines afford a sense of "stagnant time," the setting of the palace is pervaded by the "atmosphere of another age," while even "the silence was more ancient" (7). (More ancient than what? we are left to wonder.) The general, who "could only walk with the aid of a small orthopedic cart which bore his herniated testicle" (45),

The Carnivalesque-Grotesque 45

described as being "the size of an ox kidney" (11), finally expires "at an indefinite age somewhere between 107 and 232 years" (82). Nobody knows for sure. Lack of clear knowledge in virtually every arena is nonetheless continually balanced by his acting, immediately and brutally, upon little more than vague suspicion.[6] At one point, 918 heads are brought (in accordance with Rabelaisian precision) in bags for the despot's signed receipt ("signed I . . . I myself" 141). Countless others requiring corresponding receipts follow. Once the killing machine is put in motion there appears no way of stopping it. For the victims, decapitation and death are grim realities. For the general, death becomes one more subject for (unwitting) carnivalized mockery: "because the way I am I don't intend to die again, God damn it, let other people die" (36). That refrain, in turn, becomes a repeated tirade: "let other people die, God damn it" (240), while his oft-repeated final phrase, in his befuddled, clouded mind, is as close as he can come to "prayer." Himself a carnivalized figure, part of that attribution is derived from a total absence of spirit that cannot be redeemed by any corresponding fullness of what is carnal.

The dictator depicted in these pages is the clown crowned of the carnival tradition, the offspring of "a wandering bird-woman [who] at the beginning of time had given difficult birth to a no man's son who became king" (129). Fatherless, born of a mother who "had to use her lower parts to eat" (141), homeless and timeless, the ruler, whose birth marks "the beginning of time," will also see to it that "a new century of confusion and scandal was beginning in the world" (128). And that century would end, too, as the tyrant, absent (and safe) from the gala celebrations in his honor, muses: "a hundred years already, God damn it, a hundred years already, the way time passes" (202). To him the people shout (when necessary), "long live God" (137). For he is the great tyrant and the great joke of the nation.

> in bars we told the story that someone had announced to the cabinet that he had died and that they had asked each other in fright who's going to tell him, ha, ha, ha, when the truth was that it wouldn't have mattered to him if he knew it or not or he himself wouldn't have been very sure whether that street joke was true or false. [121-22]

Again, getting at the truth is not easy for "the one who gives the orders," for "God," although in this "nightmare age," the use of reason is attributed to gardenias (131), and there exists "a parrot who could guess the future" (139). Not surprisingly, in this carnivalized universe, man and beast appear to trade places within a slippery hierarchy. In *Eva Luna,* a scene is devoted to the image of a dictator's palace being taken over by the people. ("The very day the tyrant died, indigents began to take it over, timidly at first, and then in droves" Allende 1989:137.) That theme in *Autumn of the Patriarch* is expanded into an entire novel in which the indigent do not wait for the tyrant to die in order to move in, and where not only people appropriate space within those spacious quarters but so too do animals "in droves." Hence, the very first line of the novel begins: "Over the weekend the vultures got into the presidential palace." The opening passages of the novel afford the sense of the carnivalesque in a world where not only have the poor finally appropriated the belongings of the rich but animals have taken over the human sphere (as being, perhaps, in no way inferior).

> for at that time it did not look like a presidential palace but rather a marketplace where . . . orderlies [were] un-

The Carnivalesque-Grotesque

loading vegetables and chicken cages from donkeys in the corridors . . . in the midst of the uproar of tenured civil servants who found hens laying eggs in desk drawers, and the traffic of whores and soldiers in the toilets, and a tumult of birds, and the fighting of street dogs in the midst of audiences because no one knew who was who or by whom in that palace with open doors in the grand disorder of which it was impossible to locate the government. [Gárcia Márquez 1977:120]

In that "marketplace of a palace" (40), the boundaries are obliterated between inside and outside, between official (governmental) business and the business of buying and selling (vegetables or flesh), and between the human sphere and animal domain. The latter two, moreover, may at times come into their own sad conflict, as when there is noted "the uproar of the lepers and the cripples [who had appropriated the palace courtyards and passageways for their own] as they fought with the dogs over food" (217). There, too, the mother of the despot kept "water-color painted birds in public offices" (49), while painted birds "wandered about at their pleasure through salons and offices" (125). The resultant "grand disorder" of "that marketplace disaster" (12) represents of course a hallmark of the carnivalesque. Yet the presence of animals also serves as a signifier of another (sociopolitical) kind: "one January afternoon we had seen a cow contemplating the sunset from the presidential balcony, just imagine, a cow on the balcony of the nation, what an awful thing, what a shitty country" (11).

In this country, "with one-hundred-degree heat and ninety-eight-percent humidity" (148), referred to repeatedly as a perpetual "realm of gloom" (241), a despot is confused with God by a people "who don't believe in anything except life" (148) and who are perceived, in turn, only as pawns and victims. Politically perspicuous and persistent in the notion that cruelty is the best policy, the general does not recognize his own children, nor the women who bore them. In fact, he can hardly distinguish himself from his perfect double, whose assassination allows the general to perpetrate "the trick of his death" (31). In staging his own funeral, he is "horrified with the idea of being quartered and devoured by dogs and vultures amidst the delirious howls and the roar of fireworks celebrating the carnival of my death" (33). Death, in this carnivalesque work, elicits true carnival, the people's genuine street celebration—perverted, in this instance, by the death of an impostor who had served in place of a fake king. Further, in what might appear strange or paradoxical in another context, this latter fake, it turns out, cannot distinguish his own image from his real self: "I feel as if the reflection in the mirror is reversed" (217), he says, in apparent misgiving (even after the unmourned demise of his double) as to who he might be in relation to the enigma—which is himself—that even he must at times confront.

Additional falsifications abound, including the presentation (upon official instigation) of "a false dead man who arose from his grave and appeared walking on his knees through the crowd frightened by his ragged shroud and his mouth full of earth" (145), done in order to demonstrate the (equally false) healing powers of the general's dead mother in a prolonged, unsuccessful bid for her canonization. Likewise, it is falsely claimed that she had been miraculously preserved, when, in fact, "she had been stuffed according to the worst skills of taxidermy just like the posthumous animals in science museums" (146). These and other carnivalesque contrivances, conjured in the general's never-ending megalomaniacal stupor, all reduce to stark pretension, "a carnival apparatus that he himself had put together . . . a circus trick

The Carnivalesque-Grotesque 49

which he had fallen into himself without knowing it" (145). At the root of all such instances, which themselves constitute the very fabric of the work, is the guiding principle ordaining, beyond the power of the all-powerful despot, the rule of carnivalesque reversals, (death) masks, sundry dissimulations, and that great kingdom given to an even longer lasting longevity—fakedom.

In this work, which is anything but a fairy tale, the sorry figure promoted to "general of the universe" (203) sleeps in an armored room with three bars, three bolts, and three locks, which he secures at night to protect himself from all of his dominions, over which he has absolute power. Even the titles that accumulate to him resonate with their own carnivalesque effect. For "the all-worthy one who filled nature with respect and straightened the order of the universe and had taken Divine Providence down a peg" (217) seemingly has nothing better to do with his time than write on the walls of the palace toilets, "long live the general, long live the general, God damn it" (189). In those tiresome literary efforts, the general again intones that peculiar combination of a prayer and a curse in recognition of his own unprepossessing figure, which has of late fallen into incontinence, his having begun to urinate in his pants during official gatherings (238). Such behavior, of course, may signal the transformation, over time, of even the great of this world. In accordance with the spirit of the carnivalesque, however, the transformation from great to small or, better, from upper to lower, is virtually guaranteed by the unwritten, "unofficial" order of things that ensures an unenviable destiny precisely for the unwitting soul who regards himself and his works as superior and therefore safe from an unkind fate and the ravages of time.

One such case that derives as much from the realm of metaphor as from the world of the concrete is the general's "own" palace, where one cannot go without "finding a pair of lepers sleeping on the Oriental rugs in the ballroom or a blind man lost in the offices or a cripple broken on the stairs," that great "palace for the neighborhood" that has been finally, gruesomely transformed into a "house of the dead" (225-26). There only the corpse of the general can still be found wandering, lost, dragging itself through the vestiges of the vast dominion of his own unlimited power. In that dominion, governed more by a sense of cyclical, rather than linear, time, the despot himself is "fascinated by the evidence that he was living in the origins of his regime" (226), when, in fact, he is reaching the end of it: no matter the number of prayers, or curses; no matter the amount of power that has accumulated, nor the time taken to get to the end. But that cyclical recurrence of events that only leaves the dictator where he began, unloved and unloving, has taken its grim toll in all those poor souls who have been arrested, beaten, and tortured without reason, only to reveal that the victims were not evil-doers, conspirators, or enemies. Only *now*, as a result of this cruelty, they have been potentially transformed into the latter. Thus, according to the despot's criminal logic, they have to be imprisoned all over again as a new threat to his power, thereby instituting a kind of gruesome *ronde*, which is also distinctly a part of the carnivalesque.[7] Yet this carnivalesque novel, in which both what is magic and horrific play their respective, complementary roles, concludes with the end of an intolerable regime that itself closes that period of time that began with the tyrant's birth and finishes with his impossible death, as "the music of liberation and the rockets of jubilation and the bells of glory . . . announced to the world the good news that the uncountable time of eternity had come to an end" (251).

The Carnivalesque-Grotesque

The cruel dictator has finally died; his dictatorship has come to an end; the world has been transformed. Or has it? A definitive feature of the carnivalesque, as noted, is the recurrent theme of transformation. But what if transformations and reversals yield essentially the same result as had been the rule in the past? In the magnificent tapestry of *One Hundred Years of Solitude,* whose fabric is studded with glistening carnivalesque reversals, the principal protagonist begins a new revolution and a new war (amassing a grand total of thirty-two defeats) precisely at the moment when he is facing the firing squad (anticipated in the first sentence of the book) by enlisting the very same men assigned the onerous task of executing him (Gárcia Márquez 1971:127). Similarly, we read in Gárcia Márquez' *In Evil Hour* (1968): "When they hold elections again the killing will come back. . . . Always, ever since the town has been a town, the same thing happens" (1980:18). If that is the case, it does not appear to matter whether there is revolution or (democratic) evolution, since a wearisome, gruesome reality remains basically unaltered. Likewise, it appears to make no difference which new government is brought to power (or takes power). The repeated alternation from one government demanding to be taken as the "official culture," or "real" authority, to the next, requiring, in turn, the same recognition yields the same result. For the citizenry, in whom there is reflected this paradoxical alternation among constants, confusion remains the norm: "A new order reigned in the world and . . . no one . . . understood it." The "wisdom" of the "new" government is thus superseded, endlessly, by a far more reliable folk wisdom that proclaims: "Of course . . . ever since the world has been the world, no decree has ever brought any good" (117).

On the level of the fantastic, Asturias' *Mulata,* for present purposes an instructive work, provides an endless series of transformations: from poor to rich and back again; from woman into dwarf and back; from corn leaves into money; from man into stone; from man into a dwarf, back into a man, and then into a giant. Statues of saints have their heads replaced by those of animals ("and there were the saints with those animal heads"), but "suddenly," we read, "the decapitated ones recovered their true heads" (196). Does not that startling remark encapsulate a veritable truth about carnival? Are not those who are (figuratively) "decapitated" destined to recover "their true heads"? From this virtual textbook of the carnivalesque, we might well learn not only that transformations are themselves subject to reversals but that, in the process (of one thing turning into another and perhaps changing back again), they may yield nothing new. Either the new product is transformed back to the original, or the newly formed figure produces the same result as the original had done. Thus the transformation itself may appear as only a counterfeit transaction, producing nothing *of substance* that is new. Only the outer appearance changes; the inner being, the defining character, remains essentially the same.

That supposition does not represent law, of course, but only possibility—the possibility that carnival, for all its rambunctious energy, may ultimately yield the same figure as before only with a new face (or a new mask). Yet, what might appear to be an unproductive paradox may also afford a whole new range of possible understandings. Here let us chart only a few striking points within that range. First, there is still, after all, the distinct possibility within transformation for real change. At its most banal and at the same time most poignant plane, we read: "Mr. Theodore Mundstock . . . had aged a hundred years in those three since the Nazis came and spread their brown darkness over everything" (Fuks 1969:74). In its grimmest aspect, Wiesel documents an even more stark transformation thus: "During the war Michael had seen saints become criminal, all for a crust of bread—a small, dry, filthy crust could change the natural order, could reverse the structure of creation!" (1969:59). So even the sorriest semblance of sustenance (coupled, undoubtedly, with monumental hunger) can elicit a corresponding monumentally dark carnivalesque reversal in the carnivalized world of war (about which more will be said later).[8]

Second, in our consideration of what amounts, in effect, to carnivalesque transformation negating itself, it becomes evident that carnivalesque reversals may elicit the need for analogous alterations in our common understanding. Offering a hint of such thinking, Fuentes writes: "He thought about Homer, the Cid, Shakespeare: their epic dramas were written before they were lived. Achilles and Ximena, Helen, and Richard the hunchback in real life had done nothing but follow the poet's scenic instructions and act out what had already been set down. We call this inversion of metaphor 'history,' the naive belief that, first, things happen and then they are written. That was an illusion" (1992:182). Whether or not we are subject to such "naive belief" or "illusion," that brief argument surely affords the reader a carnivalesque vision of history whose intellectual impulse may go some way toward explaining why reversals or inversions can *appear* to achieve little or nothing in the end result. For, depending through which end of the telescope we choose to peer, that perception, too, is perhaps only an illusion within a series (no less) of seeming illusions, compounded oxymoron, and paradox—the complex material, after all, of which carnival is made.

Our third (already anticipated) related consideration is the considerable role played by the mask in the carnivalized work of evoking illusion—the illusion of transformation or change. In referring to the theme of the mask, Bakhtin declares that it is "the most complex theme of folk culture" (1968:39). Brief inquiry into this immense topic can nonetheless find its immediate reward. A partial resolution to the problem is suggested in Carpentier's *The Lost Steps* (1953), where the mask is perceived as representing a certain duality between man and nature. On the one hand, the mask represents "man's eternal love of the False Face, the disguise, the pre- tense of being an animal, a monster, or a malign spirit" (1979:107). Hence its adoption by popular culture. Yet the novel also speaks of nature's similar predilection for disguise, suggesting thereby the possible origins of the mask as well as the hidden rationale for its adoption by humankind: "The jungle is the world of deceit, subterfuge, duplicity; everything there is disguise, stratagem, artifice, metamorphosis" (147-48). Man appreciates the workings of this duplicity or artifice and adopts its ways to his own world. With the great promise of success that it entails, the mask, as a metaphor for nature, its designs and stratagems, thus extends from the world of nature to the human and back again in the never-ending struggle to survive that also mirrors the corresponding endless series of transformations that inspired our original inquiry.

In a sense, then, it can be argued by extension of this view that since the mask is derived in part from nature, and since it plays such a significant role in carnival, carnival too may be viewed as partly derived from the world of nature. Although carnival both represents and manifests a specifically *human* need that is likely more psychological than physiological, that need may, nonetheless, have its origins in the physical world that mandates survival first of all. Yet, as noted, this peculiar human manifestation embraces the universal effort to evoke illusion, effect at least figuratively (in both spectacle and fiction) transformations or reversals of fate and

The Carnivalesque-Grotesque

fortune, and achieve a "universal dissimulation of personality, age, demeanor, and shape" (Carpentier 1988:69) in stark contrast to the more mundane need for the usual commerce and communication.

Closely related to these crucial aspects of carnival is the circus. Its special place within the human domain is made evident by Gárcia Márquez, who charts the arrival of a circus as a moment of epiphany and awe transfixed in time, when "the whole town seemed to rise up from the earth in a miraculous silence" (1980:111). In commenting on this equally venerable human institution, whose longevity rivals that of carnival, Viacheslav Ivanov notes the significance of the circus in the artistic creativity of the twentieth century as being "the most recent continuation of the ancient carnival tradition" (1974:340). That recent continuation is wholly apparent, for example, in Rabon's *The Street,* in which circus life plays a prominent role, as a tubercular clown illustrates in true carnivalesque fashion the paradoxical power of death as a potentially regenerative force.

> It's pure comic theater.... Every evening Death gives me permission to go to the circus. Lying here all day, cut off from everything, I have begun to think that Death doesn't want to shut my impudent and sassy mouth. He—Death, that is—must be one of my greatest fans. When evening comes he takes his paws off my chest and stops choking me. He runs off to the circus and waits for me to come and make him laugh. Ha, ha, ha. He is my friend—Death, my fan.... Take my word for it, Death is curing me. [1990:122-23]

Not only is the clown a likely carnivalesque figure but, in this same novel (situated for the most part in Eastern Europe, but with an isolated passage set in China), so is the wandering Jew, who, while being perpetually an alien in a Christian world, manages to make his way to a far-flung corner of Asia, where his role remains essentially the same, only highlighted all the more. As a Japanese entrepreneur, looking to cash in on a lucky find, explains:

> Here's how it is. If appearance means anything, you have the look of a true racial Jew. In China there's a huge region whose inhabitants are Christian converts. They are very devout Christians and know the Bible exceptionally well. The fools think of themselves as very sinful. And they regard a Jew, a real Jew, as the holiest of men. In Peking, indeed, there is a small cluster of Jews, but they're not really Jews. They're Chinese, with Chinese facial features, and are the same sorts of fools. I'll take you with me to the region where the Christians live. There I'll put up a tent and send out placards announcing that a real circumcised Jew, a true great-grandson of Jesus Christ, has come and is dispensing remedies. Do you understand the scheme? There's no swindle in it; it's all according to law and truth. Isn't it true that you are a Jew? And aren't you, therefore, the grandson of Jesus Christ? [173]

And is this not just another snake oil scheme, one might well ask? Still, in this instance, where the entire premise for this carnival(esque) ploy rests on the assumption that a "true racial Jew" has been found who can be exhibited and exploited in a tent in China, we find a typical carnivalesque reversal, as the perennial pariah is thus temporarily exalted and revealed as king.

However, in an exemplary instance of the postwar novel, Kaniuk's *Adam Resurrected* (1972), which *The Street* (1928) anticipates, specifically as well as generically, the reversal of fortune that takes place occurs in the opposite direction, when the pariah, who is also a Jew and also a clown (ostensibly the most famous clown in prewar Germany), is reduced to playing the role of a dog. In this novel, the clown is exhibited on all fours, eating out of the same bowl as the master's dog. "The cook diligently prepared delicacies in honor of the distinguished guests . . . and we, Rex and me, ate our fill. They all sat at the table, we at their feet" (1972:155). As the concentration camp commandant had explained: "Your life for your clowning. A clown can pass through fire and not get burned" (141). In that latter respect, he is proved wrong: Adam emerges into "a world dispossessed of miracles" (34), after having "fooled around and played the clown in the house of death" (290), a survivor, "a weary exhausted man with a wrinkled face, with grooves crossing his cheeks, his forehead deeply lined, his body shrunken, and his entire existence humiliated" (33), because, contrary to the words of the torturer, "the insult scorches" (51). As in the earlier novel, here too the clown's "whole purpose was to blot out [for others] the fear of death" (127). And, as with the clown in *The Street,* Adam feels himself dying. "I'm sick, I'm a clown and I'm about to die, I'm dying. Bit by bit" (35). But in this later novel, the clown is motivated by the desire for death rather than life. "Inside his own heart he has purchased for himself a gravesite and he is heading right for it, non-stop" (38). Rabon's tubercular clown, in contrast, would like to make as many detours as possible. But his sojourn on the planet is, by comparison, a blessed one. His carnivalized existence does not extend, as does that of his antebellum successor, to the belief that he has "made his daughter's corpse laugh" (315).

But the ironies of the later novel are many, and so are its transformations, of which its clown protagonist is a master.

He always knew how to adjust himself like a chameleon. [159]

Adam is a man of instant transformations: from soap to distinguished citizen . . . to a dog. . . . From the genius of the circus to a swindler, from swindler to a madman in love. [160]

I'm somebody else, I'm Rex Wolfgang Adameus Stein, or Pure Adam, or Pure Pig, or Mr. Sub-human, or a man with an empty conscience, or somebody half-dead half alive. [161]

All of a sudden he calms down. He's stable. A member at a country club, a swimmer in a pool, an honorable member of the municipal museum, invited to cocktail parties at the Bolivian embassy. [186]

He can be a pauper and a millionaire, a hero and a cry-baby, drunk and sober, dead and alive, loved and hated. [188]

But the clown is not the only figure able to transform himself. The commandant, as it turns out, is equally capable once it is equally a matter of survival. In a lucid moment, he is even able to acknowledge their basic affinity (only not in terms of their common humanity): "Both of us [are] dogs, but I have a whip and you don't" (232). That instrument of dehumanization is to his mind, ironically, the only distinguishing feature between them. So, following this base "logic," at the end of the war, in the ultimate irony, he accomplishes the ultimate transformation—from victimizer to (ostensible) victim: "Here was a German doomed to live out the rest of his life as a Jew!" (83). Because, according to a more general law of reversal, enacted on the world stage, "Although the

The Carnivalesque-Grotesque 59

Germans did not know it, they were becoming hunted animals, like Jews" (Begley 1992:98), since, as Vargas Llosa puts it: "There are no limits to our deterioration" (1989:110).

Another extensive treatment of the notion of the Jew as a carnivalesque figure—as being sensitive, awkward, intelligent, pathetic, and out of place (in the most literal sense)—is effected with sympathy and humor and poignancy in Anita Desai's *Baumgartner's Bombay* (1988), in which the tragicomic protagonist, among many misadventures, is thrust into an internment camp in British-ruled India during the war years because his passport indicates that he was born in Germany and he is therefore presumed to be a full-fledged German citizen. That and similar ironies pursue this unprepossessing figure his whole life. A caring soul who administers to a sizable portion of Bombay's stray cats, Baumgartner shows a like hospitality, half a century after the Nazi horrors, to a stray Aryan, who terrorizes him and then kills him. A Nazi mentality coupled with an obvious relish for the dark side of the carnivalesque is clearly evident in the unfortunate Baumgartner's young guest, who recounts some of the bizarre practices he has witnessed in the burning ghats of Benares.

> When the fires died, the man in charge of the burning, he took up a big stick—this big—and pushed it in the fire—and took out bits of meat—human meat—that was not ash and threw it down to the riverside. All the dogs waited there—and pounced—and fought—and ate these meats—like *that,*" the boy laughed, jerking a finger at the cats. His laughter spluttered from lips that were out of control, were trembling. "And in the temples—where the priests fed the beggars—you could see some fun. I have seen even a leper with no legs, no hands, fighting a woman with his teeth—that was fun! [1990:148]

In relating his ghoulish accounts, the young stray provides two perspectives: his own excited perception of events as well as that of the greater audience, whose pleasure at witnessing horror and grief likewise remains undisguised. "The crowd waiting in the room could not have asked for more: it was all they could have desired, the drama, the theater, the raw emotions, everything. Speechless, yet audible in their horror and excitement, they watched. . . . It was wonderful, perfect. . . . All the crying anyone's heart could desire, loud and shrill and scandalous. The audience shivered with delight" (227-28).

For Wiesel, the audience is precisely the question that cannot be ignored (and is one to which we will return); it is the problem that looms over and beyond the perennial question of how one human being can treat another inhumanely. In fact, Wiesel projects the spectator's response in precisely the terms detailed by that born-too-late piece of Nazi raw material from whom we have just heard. "Ah, how pleasant"—Wiesel imagines the response of the criminal-spectator, whose crime is nothing more, or less, than his own detachment—"when they make us shiver!" (1969:170).

To be tantalized is, evidently, what is wanted. But by whom? And why? Those questions find their oblique answer in Wiesel's characterization and attendant condemnation of the spectator. "The spectator has nothing of the human in him: he is a stone in the street, the cadaver of an animal, a pile of dead wood. He is there, he survives us, he is immobile. The spectator reduces himself to the level of an object. He is no longer he, you, or I: he is 'it' " (171). He is also part of a triangle identified by Wiesel, composed of victim, executioner, and spectator, where the latter, reduced by self or circumstance to the sorry status of object, seeks to be tantalized—but at no cost to himself. In acknowledging the "mysterious bond" between victims and executioners ("they belong to the

The Carnivalesque-Grotesque   61

same universe; one is the negation of the other"), Wiesel finds this leg of the triangle the least comprehensible and perhaps the most reprehensible. "The spectator is entirely beyond us. He sees without being seen. He is there but unnoticed. The footlights hide him. He never applauds or hisses; his presence is evasive, and commits him less than his absence might. He says neither yes nor no, and not even maybe. He says nothing. He is there, but acts as if he were not. Worse: he acts as if the rest of us were not" (162).

The answer (should one be required) as to why the spectator remains condemned in this dialectic is provided in a statement of profound concern: "The injustice perpetrated in an unknown land concerns me; I am responsible. He who is not among the victims is with the executioners" (Wiesel 1967:168). On the one hand, boldly idealistic (How can one take responsibility for all that is wrong in the world?), this view is also boldly demanding (rather than gently encouraging): one *must* act in the face of persecution, cruelty, and evil, or one is (partly) to blame for the wrongdoing that results.[9] For what is blameworthy, clearly, is "the silence of the beholder, transgressing the iron law of Leviticus 5:1" (Neher 1981:142). Such, then, is the psychological and existential condition of the spectator, who, while remaining within the bounds of the law has situated himself outside those of humanity.[10]

Where does this lowly, loathsome figure come from? "The slime off the bath house wall," as the Russians say? Wiesel offers another, more inclusive but also figurative, notion. "Deep down, I thought, man is not only an executioner, not only a victim, not only a spectator: he is all three at once" (1969:174). Yet how far down must we go, one might wish to ask? Deep down in all of us, or only in some? Are these three qualities possessed in the same proportions by everyone? Or might certain people not possess any of these qualities at all? What is omitted in this seemingly facile answer to an immensely problematic issue is the possibility, even the likelihood, that there exist a few brave souls who are not encompassed by any such category and remain neither victim, nor killer, nor spectator, but "deep down"—and perhaps on the surface as well—oppose all three attitudes. And not only in thought but in deed (which is precisely what is called for in Wiesel's condemnation). But this represents another, different answer, as well as another story—the story of the partisan, the patriot, the humanist, the hero.

Finally, what Wiesel refers to as "organized cruelty" (1969: 116), that is, war itself, also bears tráits that are carnivalesque in nature. Regarding the end of the war years in Calcutta, Desai asks pointedly: "What was it—a carnival that had ended in disaster?" (1990:162). Wiesel's answer unwittingly and likely unwillingly appears to be in the affirmative. "War has fun; it overturns law and order. [Is that not an accurate, deft description of carnival?]. . . War laughs. Why not? It has every right to. It plants you in front of a stranger and says, Love him, kill him, humiliate him, and you obey without asking yourself whether it is right. An hour later you will be loved or killed or humiliated in your turn" (1967:124-25) in what amounts to the greatest possible extremes of carnivalesque reversal.

In merely broaching so profound a topic as the psychoanalysis of war, which, while conceivably a part of the subject of this book, goes far beyond its conceptual bounds, we may well ask (in accord with Wiesel) whether there is any more evident and disturbing instance of carnival, in its broad, universal, and archetypal sweep, than war—what Gárcia Márquez refers to as "the fascination of war" (1971:289)—

which demands in a moment that one kill and in the next that one be killed. In the sometimes deadly *ronde* that is also carnival, is there a more dire and fatal alternation of circumstance afforded by any other organized human activity than war? The question is aptly posed, since, at its most basic level, carnival exists as a licensed form of alternations and reversals, as a medium *designed* to "overturn law and order."[11]

As Desai bemoans in a consideration of this bleakest aspect of the carnivalesque principle of reversal that man perpetrates upon man: "Chaos was already upon them. And lunacy. The lunacy of performing acts one did not wish to perform, living lives one did not wish to live, becoming what one was not. Always another will opposed to one's own, always another fate, not the one of one's choice or even making. A great web in which each one was trapped, a nightmare from which one could not emerge" (1990:173). Chaos, lunacy, nightmare—perhaps these are the defining terms of the carnivalesque spirit subverted and contorted from its original playful aspect into its most deadly manifestation. What makes it deadly is also here underscored by the writer's insistence on the absence of choice. If choice, as existential philosophers have forcefully argued, is at the core of human existence, then submission to the demands of "organized cruelty" defines the subversion not only of the carnivalesque spirit but also of the human spirit.

In this chapter, we began with the carnivalesque and ended with the grotesque. That traversal, in effect, maps our course—which will necessarily be charted differently—through the following two chapters, devoted, respectively, to magical realism and grotesque realism. But first, in response to the question, How, in sum, may we define the carnivalesque? Let us call it, in deservedly paradoxical, oxymoronic fashion, "secular blasphemy."[12] A contradiction in terms to be sure, that phrase is meant to suggest the range of the all-encompassing expression that gives focus to this study: an irresolvable paradox that is seemingly universal and archetypal, that subverts an established value system in order to institute one of its own, that corrupts language and behavioral codes in the work of creating new ones seemingly designed exclusively to displace old ones, and that superimposes one paradox upon another until the original remains forever hidden, undisturbed, and unseen.

3 / Magical Realism

Don't be so surprised. . . . All of this is life.
—Gabriel Gárcia Márquez [1980:181]

In a single representative work of what has come to be known and appreciated worldwide as Latin American "magical realism," the following details, among numerous like pieces of information, are all presented in precise factual manner as basic reportage.

> In the country, houses were carried off by the downpour, and in one town on the coast it rained fish. [Allende 1989:24]
>
> Books, quiet during the day, opened by night so their characters could come out and wander through the rooms and live their adventures. [25]
>
> Eggs for the nation's breakfasts arrived daily by plane, producing enormous omelets on the burning asphalt of the landing strip when a crate was cracked open. [76]
>
> They could not evict the occupants because the palace and everything inside had become invisible to the human eye; it had entered another dimension where life continued without aggravation. [137]

> He knocked on every door up and down the coast, sweltering in the hot breath of the siesta, feverish in the humidity, stopping from time to time to give assistance to iguanas whose feet were stuck in the melted asphalt. [140-41]
>
> They were . . . suspicious of the paper money that today was worth something and tomorrow might be withdrawn from circulation . . . printed paper that could vanish if you turned your back—as had happened with the collection for Aid to Lepers, devoured by a goat that ambled into the treasurer's office. [141]
>
> All day they hauled mangoes, until there were none left on the trees and the house was filled to the roof-top. . . . In the days that followed, the sun beat down on the house, converting it into an enormous saucepan in which the mangoes slowly simmered; the building . . . grew soggy and weak, and burst open and rotted, impregnating the town for years with the odor of marmalade. [143]
>
> Girls wore feathers and flowers above their ears; a woman was nursing a child at one breast and a puppy at the other. [275]

In confronting that small compendium of magical realist event, one would (and perhaps should) be hard pressed to deny the possibility, even the likelihood, that at least some of what is related may well have a certain basis in reality—if not always literally, then, in some sense, figuratively. Might not iguanas, at times, require assistance? Could not a woman nurse, at one time, both a child and a puppy? Would not a goat dine on treasury notes, if given the opportunity? But let us, in any case, range no further within the murky territory of the questionable, the plausible, and the hypothetical, but acknowledge that such information, common to the "poetics of excess" that typifies magical realist texts, extends, within a broadly delineated typology, from the fantastic to the hyperbolic, and from the improbable to the possible.

While negotiating the tortuous terrain of credibility, magical realism manages to present a view of life that exudes a sense of energy and vitality in a world that promises not only joy but a fair share of misery as well. In effect, the reader is rewarded with a perspective on the world that still includes much that has elsewhere been lost: animals living in close proximity to man, close enough to devour his cash; colossal vegetation with an equally prodigious appetite, inclined to swallow all in its path—matched, for example, by Allende's scrappy survivor, Eva Luna, who is likewise "ready to devour the world" (126).

Documenting its own array of extraordinary event, supporting the notion of a peculiarly distinct Latin American reality, Alejo Carpentier's remarkable novel *The Lost Steps* relates, on a like sliding scale of credibility, the disturbing reality of perpetual political upheaval, stories of untold riches and of periodic (unrelated) inundations of butterflies and prostitutes, common beliefs that there exist "amphibious men who slept at night in the bottoms of the lakes" and that the "Amazon women really existed" (1979:129-30). Flourishing in this remarkable "corner of the world" are stories that recount the discovery of a mushroom "whose mere smell induced visual hallucinations" and a cactus "whose proximity caused certain metals to rust." Yet such tales pale before those that promise "farther ahead . . . diamonds in all the riverbeds" (126-27) and untold quantities of gold. Legends abound of the conquistadors, desperate adventures, and doomed expeditions, alongside analogous accounts of strange, unknown peoples, the creators of enormous rock formations seemingly designed to be viewed from another planet, "who had kept their records with knotted strings," killing anyone who attempted to devise a new method of retaining information. The reason these stories and beliefs persist, we are told, is that those who credit them "all lived in the vicinity of the jungle"—adjacent, that is, to "The Unknown" (130-31), "the least explored area of the planet" (128), where the sense that seemingly anything can happen inevitably allows for the flourishing of corresponding beliefs. Hence the nature of the place naturally propagates strange tales of the place. "Here we were . . . on the threshold of the unknown, in the proximity of possible wonders" (133)—where "possible" is instantly transformed into probable, as we are transported from the domain of the real to the magically real by the similarly uncharted stratagems of the artistic imagination.

Yet integrated within this self-reflexive art form can be found a miniature poetics of magical realist narrative, an abbreviated source book documenting the common detail of a complex reality—ethnographic, geographic, climatic, historic, mythologic, and cosmologic—that contributes to the making of uncommon art. ("A sight you can't imagine, when you see the Andes turn into jungle, covered with vegetation, animals, mist. Ruins everywhere. . . . A land of condors, snow, clear sky, jagged, ocher peaks." Vargas Llosa 1989:127, 134) An exemplary case in point, illustrating what is essentially a critical effort on the part of the novelist to provide a tentative poetics of magical realism, is instanced in Allende's *Of Love and Shadows* (1984).

> He also lost himself in literature; seduced by the work of Latin American writers, he realized he lived in a country in miniature, a spot on the map, buried in a vast and marvelous continent where progress arrives several centuries late: a land of hurricanes, earthquakes, rivers broad

Magical Realism 69

> as the sea, jungles where sunlight never penetrates, where mythological animals creep and crawl over eternal humus alongside human beings unchanged since the beginning of time; an irrational geography where you can be born with a star on your forehead, a sign of the marvelous; an enchanted realm of towering cordilleras where the air is thin as a veil, of absolute deserts, dark, shaded forests, and serene valleys. Here all races are mixed in the crucible of violence: feathered Indians; voyagers from faraway lands; itinerant blacks; Chinese stowed like contraband in apple crates; bewildered Turks; girls like flames; priests, prophets, and tyrants—all elbow to elbow, the living as well as the ghosts of those who through the centuries trod this earth blessed by seething passions. These American men and women are everywhere, suffering in the cane fields; shivering with fever in the tin and silver mines; lost beneath the water, diving for pearls; surviving against all odds, in prisons. [1988:205]

In this telling passage, we see a profound preoccupation with the land and the earth; with the multifarious creatures, including the great variety of humankind, that populate this vast, still only partly explored realm; the intermingling of the real with the surreal (or magically real), affording the celebration of a rich sphere replete with incomparable possibility. Acknowledging in its opening frame the human capacity to become "lost" in the bright wonderment of literature, the passage also recognizes in its concluding phrase the eminent potential for being lost to oneself and others in the darkness of prison. This is a world rich in potential and fraught with danger. Only the adventurous need journey here; only the tenacious will survive. In effect, Allende offers the reader in an encapsulated, essentially critical mode the sources of magical realism as a literary form. Permeating these few lines, as well as the literature as a whole, is the need—against great odds imposed as much by historical and political upheaval as by natural event—to survive. Survival, after all, is an overriding theme. And one possible mode of self-preservation is to engage the realm of the creative imagination.

For the writer, this may be achieved by reenacting in a heightened, more conscious fashion the role of the child in perceiving the world and everything in it as remarkable and new. Magical realism's most far-reaching origin is perhaps rooted in the remembrance of childhood, with its attendant wonder at the splendor of the world, whose multitudinous variety of actual and potential manifestations within it engenders extraordinary corresponding flights of the human imagination. In Allende's *Eva Luna,* however, we see how significant is the role of perspective: what is magical for some is ordinary for others. "The journey began by canoe, down tributaries that wound through a landscape to derange the senses, then on muleback over rugged mesas where the cold freezes night thoughts, and finally in a truck, across humid plains through groves of wild bananas and dwarf pineapple and down roads of sand and salt; but none of it surprised the girl, for any person who first opens her eyes in the most hallucinatory land on earth loses the ability to be amazed" (1989:5). Yet, as a counterpoint to such "loss," the young heroine also learns from her mother "that reality is not only what we see on the surface; it has a magical dimension as well" (22).

That "magical dimension" is hypostatized in literature by the superimposition of one perceived reality upon another, as seemingly fantastic events that may nevertheless appear to the indigenous, heterogeneous peoples of the region as an indubitable norm are embedded within what outsiders perceive as distinct, exclusive, and the only "true" reality. ("Our world seems like a fable to the people [of Europe] because they've lost their sense of the fabulous." Carpentier 1988:123) This absolute disjuncture in basic perceptions of the world is situated at the core of a transnational literature designed to account for events and possibilities that are immanent, even uniquely inherent, to the southern hemisphere of the Americas, where the intrusion of the jungle into city life is an ever-present threat; where the mix of different peoples, with their various myths and beliefs, fomenting like intrusions into the business of daily life, results in remarkable blendings and certain tensions; and where those tensions are manifested in perpetual political conflict.

Magical realist texts derive from a host of Latin American realities. Among the more apparent sources are an imposing geography, composed of daunting natural barriers—impenetrable forests, dangerous waters, and portentous heights—and a frequently unbearable humid Caribbean atmosphere that inevitably dampens the spirits. The geographical proximity of the jungle to the city elicits a related omnipresent sense of the closeness of the prehistoric past to modern life, of myth, or primordial thinking, to scientific thought.[1] Yet that closeness, filtered through a creative human imagination nurtured on a mix of the traditions and beliefs of the native Indians, as well as those of the transplanted Africans and Europeans absorbed into that world of prolific cultural hybridization, allows for a seemingly inevitable portrayal of the fantastic as factual and realistic.

On the first page of *Eva Luna,* we are given a clear sense of the great proximity of the primordial past to modern life: "I came into the world with a breath of the jungle in my memory." Inherent to that (collective) memory is the complicity of myth and history, legend and "reality"—a complicity that is likewise signaled on the novel's opening page, with its recognition of that "enchanted region where for centuries adventurers have searched for the city of pure gold the conquistadors saw when they peered into the abyss of their own ambitions" (Allende 1989:1). Such juggling in the collective memory of "a breath of the jungle," accompanied by a haunting companion recollection of "the conquistador without conquest" (Fuentes 1992:30), tearing through that jungle (and through the native people's fabric of life) in search of the fabled El Dorado, represent twin, linked sources of magical realism. The image of an all-encompassing, "enchanted region," where "time is bent and distances deceive the human eye" (Allende 1989:2), is perhaps most graphically depicted in *The Lost Steps*.

> For a century a grim struggle went on with the jungle, expeditions that ended in tragic failure, wandering in circles, eating saddle leather, drinking the blood of their horses, dying the daily death of St. Sebastian shot through with arrows. This was the story of the known attempts, for the chronicles fail to mention the names of those small groups who had burned their wings in the flame of the myth and left their skeletons in armor at the foot of some unscalable wall of rock. [Carpentier 1979:128-29]

Just such an assumption—that the chronicles have sinned through omission—makes of "this prenatal world" (179) an unparalleled myth-propagating domain in which the historical fact of the Spanish invasion is forever intermeshed with fantasies of gold.[2] As a result of such tantalizing speculation, history and legend, myth and reality remain inextricably intertwined, making the days of the conquistadors still seem vital and alive.

Likewise, just as the borders between fact and fiction remain intriguingly blurred, the people who bear this collective memory—themselves representing extraordinary mixtures of Indian, African, and European blood—embody traits that cannot be traced to a single source or comprehensible point of origin. Thus Eva Luna's mother is unable to tell her daughter of her own origins. Yet we know precisely how Eva came into the world and how she got her name: "Her father belonged to the Luna tribe, the Children of the Moon. Let it be Luna, then. Eva Luna" (Allende 1989:21). But is it not a kind of "lunacy" (a historical, much documented lunacy) to want to convert such people as belong to the moon? And do not such efforts at conversion—from one faith to another, from one presumed (primitive) state to another condition presumed more civilized—serve also to characterize this "most hallucinatory land on earth?" For as its generic history repeatedly documents, the once paradoxically brutal intrusion of missionary priests (accompanied by soldiers) into the lives of natives, whose faith is deeply rooted in primordial beliefs, remains a still common (but more peaceable) event bearing a certain universal stamp.

Crucial to the way this "hallucinatory" impression is maintained of a land where "time is bent," and in which the real is forever wedded to what is magically real, is the manner by which time is perceived and chronicled—by modern man, as opposed to his primitive counterpart, in whom there is no corresponding mania for measuring the passage of time.[3] That the way time is perceived in the magical realist text is bound to be skewed is inadvertently but convincingly argued by Eva Luna: "While you and I are speaking here, behind your back Christopher Columbus is inventing America, and the same Indians that welcome him in the stained-glass window are still naked in a jungle a few hours from this office, and will be there a hundred years from now" (300-301). Her implicit argument for the principle of simultaneity affording a viable conception of time, mirrors, in effect, the theoretical view propounded by Leach: "But if there is nothing in the principle of the thing, or in the nature of our experience, to suggest that time must necessarily flow past at constant speed, we are not required to think of time as a constant flow at all. Why shouldn't time slow down and stop occasionally, or even go into reverse?" (1961:133).[4] In thematic, literary terms that provide a carnivalesque potential for temporal reversal and inversion, magical realism poses essentially the same questions.

Time is thus frequently presented as cyclical, rather than linear. What occurs on one occasion (which is not likely to be the first) is destined to take place again on another, perhaps different, plane. The result is the ready potential for a kind of "eternal recurrence," whose principle aspect, however, is rooted more in dire repetition than in an implicit acknowledgment of eternity. Revolution, for instance, appears bound to recur ("You go on believing in writs. These days . . . justice doesn't depend on writs; it depends on bullets" Gárcia Márquez 1980:173); but the promise of a better life in the future made on each occasion of political upheaval is rarely (if ever) realized. Thus, irony and paradox remain rooted in ever-recurrent social and political aspiration: "Fascinated, she drew maps, made lists, imagined strategies—totally overlooking the risks—believing in her heart that, like so many other things in the nation's history, nothing would go beyond the planning stages" (Allende 1989:271).

An arresting mix of the real and fantastic, time, in this genre, also bears a magical quality that extends beyond the mundane considerations of war preparations (and their eternal recurrence) to a starkly contrastive fixed tableau that is stunningly but dispassionately captured in the following spare account of what might naturally be taken as a common event.

> Some stated that near the mouth of that volcano disappearing from sight behind the lower peaks eight members of a scientific expedition lay encrusted in ice as in a show window; they had succumbed half a century before. They sat in a circle, in a state of suspended animation, just as death had transfixed them, gazing out from the crystal that covered their faces like a transparent death mask. [Carpentier 1979:77]

Thus, time that (for us) never stops may yet remain stationary.[5]

In magical realism, we find ancient mythologies (designed in part to account for the problem of time) taking their place alongside contemporary issues. As a generic contemporary literary form, construed in part from the mythologies and cosmologies of indigenous Indian tribes, magical realism is derived from a bundle of traits bearing what Vargas Llosa terms a "magico-religious mentality" (1990:158). That phrase is repeatedly invoked in his novel *The Storyteller* (1987) for its special quality as a signifier entailing a wide range of shifting signifieds, which collectively bear the potential for a multitude of related meanings that are all nonetheless centered on a mythological (rather than a scientific) understanding of the world and man's place within it.

Inherent, then, within the seemingly oxymoronic expression "magical realism," itself designating a highly proliferated and equally variegated form, Indian mythology and contemporary event not only exist tangentially but may also interpenetrate one another providentially. That is, what happens to the man of civilization in such works may well be derived from what belongs to the lore of his Indian counterpart. The providence of the one thus helps determine the fate of the other. In this literature, reflective of and concerned with modern man's lack of a guiding philosophy or cosmology, that of his more "primitive" brethren serves, in effect, to direct their fate. In Bakhtinian terms, the word of the other serves to define the (essentially absent) word of the self—where the self is the modern *arriviste* and the other is the indigenous native, whose word is his myth and his faith.

Yet that "newcomer" is not entirely bankrupt either. A principal theme of *Eva Luna* is the modern literary imagination—its sources and profound effects. Among other concerns and preoccupations, this is a book about how and why literature is made. A storyteller herself, first of all, Eva Luna meticulously explains the origins and manner by which her stories are created. ("Often only a word or two would string together a rosary of images in my mind." Allende 1989:73) She regards her gift humbly but understands intuitively the great human need for stories in our lives (even if we cannot rationally explain that need). For her, the story exists "to make our journey through life less trying" (22); "to put a little order in that chaos, to make life more bearable" (301). In effect, *Eva Luna* affords a miniature *ars poetica,* an explanation or rationale, for the making of verbal art. The story provides comfort and consolation to those in need (260-61); it is a "pure" art form that exists as "a game of infinite possibilities" (153) in which one "had only to speak the right word to give it life" (188); it creates "myth" as a way of explaining life—or providing someone in need with a life story ("because mine is filled with blood and lamentation, and I cannot use it in my way through life" 281). In this novel, the story is a gift of love transmitted from one soul to another.

Eva Luna also explains: "I could see an order to the stories stored in my genetic memory since my birth" (251). That vision removes the art of storytelling from the domain of individual creation and places it in a different realm—one that corresponds with the beliefs held by the indigenous peoples of the land that is explored, as a kind of anthropological literary investigation, in *The Storyteller*. In treating the ancient art of storytelling on two levels, this novel acknowledges the story form in its implicit modern sense, as a literary mode that is left open to interpretation. But more significantly, this work examines the realm of primordial thinking, in which, by contrast, the story bears intrinsic worth as a message that is immediately grasped for its spiritual content: "Storytelling can be something more than mere entertainment. . . . something primordial, something that the very existence of a people may depend on" (Vargas Llosa 1990:94). Because, as Asturias explains: "In this world it's not necessary for everybody to know everything. A few know and the rest are satisfied with listening to them" (1982:110).

Structured in a way that clearly integrates principles of ancient cosmogony with contemporary philosophical quest, *The Storyteller* presents the reader with two kinds of ancient story: legend and myth. The former represents what amounts essentially to tribal lore. It is a story that fascinates and intrigues its listeners, even when—and perhaps because—it is told over and over again. While myth also partakes of the past, it is designed primarily to take account of the elements, the plant and animal world, the earth and the heavens, in such a way as to explain the world and its many facets, as well as the place of human beings within that complex aggregate. From one authoritative perspective on this vast topic, myth, "in its living primitive form, is not merely a story told but a reality lived . . . it is a living reality, believed to have once happened in primeval times, and continuing ever since to influence the world and human destinies" (Malinowski 1954:100). Legend, by contrast, plays a less significant role. It is thus upon myth (rather than legend) that tribal cosmogony is based, offering the potential for recurrence that is also renewal. "Thanks to the things you tell us, it's as though what happened before happens again, many times" (Vargas Llosa 1990:61). This perception of recurrence, in contrast to the dreary repetition of current (political) event, offers not so much hope for a better world as the consolation that this world is the best possible—because all these good things keep happening repeatedly without end.

In reiterated references to "minute primitive cultures scattered throughout the . . . Amazon" (13), *The Storyteller* argues implicitly that ancient myth and ritual have had a profound effect on both Latin American literature and culture—the latter term defined simply and intelligently as "a way of looking at things" (147). That way of looking, for primitive man, is through myth. Myth explains the world and "our" place within it. Myth attempts to designate "where before ended and after began" (116). It tells of the beginning of time, of the courtship of the sun and the moon, how the earth came into being, why man began to "walk" or wander the earth (in order to help the sun remain in the sky—for if people were to remain in one place for too long, the sun might fall). Myth affords an understanding of the universe that is causal. "Nothing that happens happens just because. . . . There's a reason for everything; everything is a cause or a result of something" (202).[6] This "primitive" point of view clearly exists in polar opposition to contemporary notions of an absurdist world. Perhaps best illustrating this polarity are the juxtaposed notions "synthetic" and "authentic," in which opposition the latter term suggests the idea of "life moving to a primordial rhythm" (Carpentier 1979:153), the sense of community life, where everyone fulfills his appointed task in harmony with others, and where every task performed is *essential* in the most fundamental sense of preserving life.

The Storyteller addresses the issue of the original power and importance of the story as a profound cultural entity, while the storyteller himself performs a critical role as "the memory of the community." He represents a living source of what Jung calls the "collective unconscious"—the cultural memory that had resided in every individual at a time when such memory was still conscious. "Using the simplest, most time-hallowed of expedients, the telling of stories," the storyteller provides "the living sap that circulated [making individuals] into a society, a people of interconnected and interdependent beings" (Vargas Llosa 1990:93). This view extends beyond the human sphere to express a vision of a unified world, typified by a set of mutual dependencies among all its species. What is known and understood and not forgotten is thus the unity of the world—the principle upon which Creation was founded. As Carpentier explains in a like context: "Creation is no laughing matter, and they all knew this instinctively and accepted the role each of them had been assigned in the great tragedy of living. But it was a tragedy with a unity of time, place, and action" (1979:171). For the tribal mentality, to be deprived of that clear, irrefutable sense of (classical) unity would be equivalent to being plunged without salvation into the darkest depths of a carnival world replete with all manner of horrors for which there is no possible attendant explanation.

By fulfilling their assigned role in Creation, "in the great tragedy of living," however, they avoid the greater tragedy of a hopelessly carnivalized world, which is Chaos. Their simple, life-embracing perspective might be formulated thus: "We don't have any words of our own, and that's why we repeat the words people speak to us" (Asturias 1982:110). Most prominent in helping them to understand their role and their place in the world is the storyteller, a man of limited possessions ("But what do I have? The things I'm told and the things I tell, that's all." Vargas Llosa 1990:119) but of rare understanding. The relationship between him and his people is both simple and profound. "Here we are. I in the middle, you all around me. I talking, you listening. We live, we walk. That is happiness, it seems" (40). Yet a similarly rewarding, essentially dialogical principle is likewise in effect in the more sophisticated world of Eva Luna, where she tells her stories to a similarly appreciative (and spiritually needy) audience. So, the role of the story in both the primordial and the modern world appears essentially the same—to guide, enrich, enlighten—although in tribal society its function is formalized. In addition, their subject matter and the manner of their telling are necessarily different. For while Eva Luna relates engaging fictions, the storyteller is articulating Truth.

> The things you'd least expect speak. There they are: speaking. Bones, thorns. Pebbles, lianas. Little bushes and budding leaves. The scorpion. . . . The butterfly with rainbow wings. The hummingbird. . . . One and all have something to tell. That is, perhaps, what I have learned by listening. . . . I learned the story of some of the animals from them. They had all been men, before. They were born speaking, or, to put it a better way, they were born from speaking. Words existed before they did. And then, after that, what the words said. Man spoke and what he said appeared. That was before. Now a man who speaks speaks, and that's all. Animals and things already exist. That was after. [131-32]

This encapsulated view offers an edifying cosmogony in which time is registered by two markers, Before (signifying Chaos) and After (indicating Harmony). It also suggests a remarkable semiotics whereby the signified is born of the signifier. In (unwitting) accordance with biblical teaching, in the beginning was the Word. But from the Word, in this mode of primitive thinking, is born the world, with man as the creator who authors the world and every living thing in it by virtue of a once God-like, prolific imagination. Man the author of words is also man the creator of the world. In the beginning was the word, man's word, and from his word emerged the world. This view amounts to a secular religion that makes man the creator and (through a similarly skewed semiotics) his signifier the progenitor. From the word of man is born the world of other living creatures. So, we might say: "That's where before ended and after began" (116).

Remarkably, by refracting events of recent European history through the prism of ancient South American myth, we note that the literature of the Holocaust observes essentially the same two designates: before and after the horror that has stained with blood the history of mankind for all time. From the cosmogonic perspective of the tribe, we find prehistory divided into a *before* that is made tenable only in terms of myth, whose sole purpose is to provide for an *after* that is still comprehensible. Through an extraordinary inversion, the history of modern man is also divided into before and after— only, in our terrible case, the reverse is the result: we can more or less understand the world before the war; but since that cataclysm, as a result of the preponderance of horrific information embracing that virtually all-encompassing experience, we are at a loss to understand our own *after*.[7]

In extreme formulation, perhaps the most insidious effect of the war experience was to deprive primitive man's successors of faith, certitude, a belief in the potential viability of myth. ("His memorable scenes are the stuff of nightmares, not myth." Begley 1992:2) If myth affords such joyous expression as "This is my world. This is my home. The best thing that ever happened to me is living here, on this earth" (Vargas Llosa 1990:122), then what words might the twentieth-century concentration camp victim articulate that are comparable? That are equally viable, or credible? That are as joyful and grateful? Instead we read: "Death will follow us all our lives, wherever we go. There'll be no more peace for us" (Appelfeld 1983:160). Not only are victims deprived of such expression, of the possibility of felicitous reminiscence—which, in a collective sense, defines myth as the union of story and memory—but all of humankind cognizant of recent history are likewise deprived. Otherwise put, in a very different context (in which the tribe bemoans its own loss of wisdom) but in entirely appropriate terms: "We don't even know what the harmony that exists between man and [the world] can be, since we've shattered it forever" (Vargas Llosa 1990:100).

If, as we are told in Vargas Llosa's novel, a display of anger on the part of a single individual, can, in the view of one gentle tribal cosmology, disturb the balance and harmony of the world,[8] then what do we make of the magnitude of that astounding, incomprehensible display that is twentieth-century historical event? How are we to understand its incomparable deleterious effect?

In *The Storyteller,* we read that "an ancestral instinct impelled [the tribe] irresistibly toward a life of wandering, scattered them through the tangled virgin forests" (104). In Aharon Appelfeld's *To the Land of the Cattails* (1984), a woman returning to her birthplace, after many years away from home, imagines her childhood world as a place characterized by "man and nature dwelling in harmony" (1986:82). Instead of that expected harmony, and although, we are told, "there was something religious in that return" (129), she is greeted at the end of her quest by a grim irony, having arrived home just in time to be sent off on one last journey, as part of the first deportations to the Nazi death camps. That irony is profoundly compounded at the end of the novel when a crowd of innocents simply congregate, virtually unguarded, at a provincial railroad station in Eastern Europe, "separated from their loved ones, forgotten, waiting for a train to come and take them" (139). ("The platform was bustling with sub-humanity on its way to extermination." Kaniuk 1972:159) They wait in fear, uncertainty, and dread. "We didn't know what to do, so we came here" (Appelfeld 1986:140). In complicity with horrendous historical fact, and in ignorance of the evil that awaits them, these human sojourners in cattle cars instinctively follow (like their primitive brethren) a perhaps primordial inclination to be with their own people.[9] So, at the end, "an old locomotive . . . went from station to station, scrupulously gathering up the remainder" (148). The human remnant: what more frightening oxymoron or more sinister irony can there be?

Yet, oddly, a seeming universe and light years away, that same pathetic phrase applies, *mutatis mutandis,* to the indigenous peoples of Latin America. For, if Appelfeld's work tells of gross human extermination, Vargas Llosa's tale speaks of cultural annihilation. Or, as Allende puts it in referring to the native tribes and their history: "That had been their lot for the last five hundred years: persecution and extermination" (1989:283).

Vargas Llosa's *The Storyteller* and Carpentier's *The Lost Steps* share a common element: both recount a return—to the jungle, to a world that is primitive, to a people whose thought is rooted in the primordial. Exemplifying such thought, an anecdote is related in the former work about how a prisoner of one tribe is permitted to wander around freely in the village of his captors. "His dog, however, was shut up in a cage and was watched very closely. Captors and captive were evidently in agreement as to the symbolic import of this; in the minds of both parties the caged animal kept the prisoner from running away and bound him to his captors more securely—the force of ritual, of belief, of magic—than any iron chain could have" (Vargas Llosa 1990:78-79). That "force" derives in part from an innate appreciation of the mutual reliance between man and animal that had prevailed in primitive society. Equally important, it derives from a literal understanding of the principle of contiguity, now understood primarily in figurative terms but illustrated in this little account as concrete, affording the potential for real application in the actual world of primitive man.[10] An obvious interpretation allows us to observe that, in this line of thought, the man remains "bound" to his dog. Likewise, whole communities remain bound by thinking that takes literally such notions as "community," "society," or "group" that might otherwise remain only abstractions.

In both novels, the principal character goes back in time—in *The Lost Steps* ostensibly to search for the origins of music, in *The Storyteller* to investigate the origins of narrative. But what is actually discovered in both works are people who "live in harmony with the natural world" (242). Curiously, to say that the respective protagonists enter a "different world" appears not so much metaphorical as literal. For each novel, on several levels, breaks down the common understanding of the distinctions between literal and figurative, concrete and metaphoric—in the sense that each reveals a fundamental *lack* of such distinctions in primitive thinking. For the native tribe, all linkages are *real* rather than only imagined or supposed. Further, in both its temporal and its spatial aspects, the world described in each affords a novelized, documentary account that contrasts past and present. Yet the past still exists in the present, yielding, paradoxically, a present that may not be properly able to account for time. In part, this paradox may be explained by a brief passage in *Eva Luna:* "All ages of history co-exist in this immoderate geography. While in the capital entrepreneurs conduct business affairs by telephone with associates in other cities on the globe, there are regions in the Andes where standards of human behavior are those introduced five centuries earlier by the Spanish conquistadors, and in some jungle villages men roam naked through the jungle, like their ancestors in the Stone Age" (Allende 1989:178). Clearly, the "coexistence" of these monumentally different time periods in human development precludes a general consensus on the part of those living as entrepreneurs in one period or roaming naked in the other as to how such basic expressions as "then" and "now" are to be conceived, independently and in relation to one another.

In Carpentier's novel, time and space are crucial (beyond being the principal compositional elements of any narrative work), in the sense that both are explored for their interrelated metaphysical as well as existential qualities. The trip is made back in time and deep into the jungle—to a place that still exists before time, before there was even a sense of how to chronicle time. The work juxtaposes the very distant past with the present, the contemporary world with the prehistoric. In those juxtapositions, our times appear insufficient; the modern world does not stack up against its prehistoric counterpart.

This is true in part because the journey represents the repeated encounter with raw life, where one is confronted by "an endless wall of trees standing trunk to trunk," where the air is so thick it seems filled with plankton, and where the depths of caves seem "a slimy tangle of snakes" (Carpentier 1979:141-43). This is life at its most prolific, the dawn of creation, when one is afraid at night and rejoices at the light of dawn, with its promise of a new day and new wonders in a world that is itself still new.[11]

This novel documents the spatial journey of its hero into the jungle matched by an attendant temporal displacement into the past. (He "now saw the breathtaking possibility of traveling in time as others travel in space." 158) On a superficial level, the trip into the past represents a single, individualist effort to recover one's roots and heritage. But as the protagonist penetrates deeper into the jungle from chapter to chapter, it becomes a trip into the past of all mankind—to that generic place from which we have all emerged. In this tale that evolves, therefore, as supra-individual,[12] we see (as in *The Storyteller*) the terrible gulf in values that exists between modernity and the prehistoric. Contemporary culture is portrayed as devoid of true meaning; we have lost the sense of ourselves, the earth, and our place in relation to it. Ritual is no longer comprehended but only practiced mindlessly, ritualistically, rather than meaningfully. We live a life of shadows behind which is a far richer, more substantial reality that goes unperceived. Curiously, this dire message is communicated through a governing artistic principle that is carnivalesque at base. For a return to the prehistoric represents a carnivalesque reversal of the temporal order.

The carnivalesque implies reversal—which is implemented by the physical reality of the world of magical realism, affording a *realistic* sense of a world turned upside down, where day and night, for instance, appear interchangeable. Going back in time in *The Storyteller* means traveling "along narrow river channels so choked with tangled vegetation overhead that in broad daylight it seemed dark as night" (Vargas Llosa 1990:72). Similarly, when the sky is darkened in *The Lost Steps* by an inundation of butterflies, we are told that "these swarms of butterflies were nothing new in the region, and that when they took place the sun was almost blotted out for the whole day" (Carpentier 1979:121). This is simply a *fact* of the place and is therefore told in a matter-of-fact way. But such facts nonetheless lend themselves to the carnivalesque attitude and its application in literature.

Within this same category of "basic truths" that afford the carnivalesque a healthy grip on whatever tale emerges from these seemingly documented "facts" is the reality of revolution—of repeated political upheaval in this part of the world, "this continent of Indians and Negroes who spend their time making revolutions to overthrow one dictator and install another" (Allende 1986:70).[13] In Carpentier's novel (and numerous others within the Latin American tradition), just as the various settings (the cities and towns, the jungle) are essentially generic to South America, so is the seemingly never-ending battle for a political ideal. "It seemed that the radio stations were broadcasting the victory of the winning party and the jailing of the members of the previous government. In this country, I was told, passing from power to prison was the normal thing" (1979:60).[14] That "normal thing," of course, is not normal by any common standard, but it does fall within the common framework of the carnivalesque, which, by its very nature and origins, seeks to project a "gay" sense of approval in response to the unforseen reversal of fortune and power. In fact, carnival originates in the popular projection of precisely such reversals (or "inversion of bipolar opposites" [Ivanov 1984:11], as more formal semiotic expression would have it).

Paradoxically, we frequently find in Latin American letters a nearly comic response, a clear reflection of the carnival attitude, to the depiction of revolution—a generic historical fact that nearly always costs lives. That grim fact is accounted for in equally grim terms by Vargas Llosa in *The Real Life of*

Alejandro Mayta (1984), a work that explores the psychological workings and correspondent political activity of the omnipresent revolutionary mentality: "There is an essential ingredient, always present in the history of this country, from the most remote times: violence. Violence of all kinds: moral, physical, fanatical, intransigent, ideological, corrupt, stupid—all of which have gone hand in hand with power here. And that other violence—dirty, petty, low, vengeful, vested, and selfish—which lives off the other kinds" (1989:109). Yet, in counterpoint to such a stark observation, this same novel partakes greatly of the carnivalesque in depicting its central, pivotal event: the novelistic investigation and eventual "revelation" of a travestied, carnivalized attempt at revolution in which, among other ludicrous flukes, foibles, and failings, the four adults and seven adolescents who attempt to perpetrate what all the same amounts to an abortive, violent governmental purge must commandeer a taxi for their venture, since not a one of these amateur perpetrators knows how to drive. Thus, in exploring the nature of violent government upheaval as a seeming way of life (or death), the novel nonetheless continually veers into the dark side of carnival. "I guess he's dead, probably someone killed him, because the way things have been going . . . no one dies of old age anymore. Somebody kills you. And you never know who" (233).

In *The Campaign,* which likewise explores the theme of seemingly endless revolution, Fuentes, too, frequently presents dire events in carnivalesque terms: "There he was, under orders . . . to establish relations with a series of cruel, haughty, audacious, smilingly fraternal, egoistic warlords, who all felt they had a right to take anything—ranches, lives, women, crops, Indians, horses . . . in the name of independence" (1992:68). In this carnivalized world, women, whose "disorderly conduct" is duly noted and "who confused the war of independence with a campaign of prostitution" (76), fare no better (or worse) than their male counterparts: "The women opted for the most fiery party, joining the ranks of independence as a 'pretext to abandon religion and modesty, and to give themselves over to pleasure' " (67). So, as Fuentes sums things up in a kind of offhanded pithyness, which frequently reveals a flash of the carnivalesque: "Everyone exploited, everyone recruited, everyone pillaged" (68). While the whole thing is explained (if ever it can be) in such perplexed, comic, Gogolian pronouncements as these: "There's a revolution, some kind of dumb business. . . . An abortive coup, something like that. . . . Things start off as a demonstration and end up as a revolution" (Vargas Llosa 1988:268, 298).[15]

In *The Lost Steps,* Carpentier achieves a certain remarkable balance in his depiction of just that kind of "demonstration." On the one hand, we see a small (unnamed) part of Latin America erupt in violence, shooting, and war. Illustrated at the same time, in carnivalized fashion, is the "fact" that during this time of upheaval in the world of man, the insect world finds an opportunity to stage its own revolt. "It was as though a subterranean world had suddenly come alive, dredging up from its depths a myriad of strange forms of animal life. Out of the gurgling waterless pipe came queer lice, moving gray wafers . . . little centipedes that curled up at the slightest alarm. . . . Inquiring antennae, whose body remained invisible, reached suspiciously out of the faucets" (1979:57). Thus we find depicted two parallel insurgencies: one affords a telling account of the blood and gore and horror yielded by the unrestrained use of guns and bullets; the other, in construing the nature of the place, provides a carnivalized sense of the correspondence between the human revolution and the insect revolt. "A few hours of neglect, of man's vigilance relaxed, had sufficed in this climate for the denizens of the slime to take over the beleaguered stronghold via the dry water pipes" (57).

Perhaps a viable way to explain both the insects and the revolution is in the semantically loaded (if grammatically weak) injunction: "Here, jungle!" (58). The natural environment, then, literally and figuratively breeds insects and foments political upheaval. "The conductor had been killed by a spent bullet that struck him in the temple as he stood carelessly by the window in his room. . . . The flies were everywhere now, buzzing around the lights, crawling on the walls, getting entangled in the women's hair. Outside the carrion was multiplying" (64). What makes this picture of revolution so convincing and awful is Carpentier's insistent intermeshing of insect imagery with the human carnage.

Similarly, Rulfo's *Pedro Paramo,* with its emphasis squarely placed upon the carnival play between life and death (discussed earlier), displays a like carnivalized attitude toward revolution and its frequently unschooled practitioners, as shown in the following exchanges. In each instance, the *patron* (whose name gives title to the work) confronts fighting men (his own and others), all of whom are united only by their common uncertainty as to what to make of the current political situation, the resultant instability, and their own respective roles in it all.

> "And tell those men I'll be waiting for them whenever they have time. What kind of revolutionaries are they?"
> "I don't know. They just said that that's what they're called." [Rulfo 1969:92]

> "As you see, we've taken up arms."
> "And?"

Magical Realism

> "That's all. Isn't that enough?"
> "But why have you done it?"
> "Because a lot of others have done the same thing. Didn't you know about it? We're waiting till we get instructions, and then we'll know what it's all about. For the time being, we're here."
> "I know what it's about," another one said, "and if you'd like I'll tell you. We've rebelled against the government and against people like you because we're sick of putting up with you. Because the government is rotten and because you and your kind are just stupid crooks and bandits. I won't say any more about the government because we're going to do our talking with bullets." [95]
>
> "Where are they from?"
> "From the north. They wreck everything they find. They're so strong I don't think anybody can beat them."
> "Why don't you join up with them, then? I've already told you to join whoever's winning." [106]

The sense of confusion, on the one hand, can be outrageous: "There was no one to shoot at in this phantasmagorical campaign" (Fuentes 1992:67). On the other, the impression of a history pockmarked by bullets and unrelenting violence also finds its place. In the perennially confusing context of one governmental declaration affirming the establishment of a new "official" order in the face of endlessly repeated like assertions, and thus resulting in a carnivalesque series of political transformations, we find the telling remark: "It's a question, if one might say so . . . of a case of terrorism in the moral order" (Gárcia Márquez 1980:115). That "case," while documented in magical realism, finds its most egregious realization in grotesque realism.

Although a hallmark of Latin American magical realism is its presentation, unparalleled in world literature, of felicitous possibility coupled with astounding event, there is nonetheless the frequent intrusion of the dark side of life into the much celebrated bright. Isabel Allende's *Of Love and Shadows* well illustrates the point. Within its pages, we also find the usual outlandish trappings of magical realism: a "carnival of insignificant wonders," including "the possessed . . . the spooked, the damned, the loonies, [who] were there in abundance" (1988:63). There are also certain peculiar "wonders" specific to this novel: a girl who can spit tadpoles, a deaf mute who is able to stop a watch by looking at it, and the "never-before-seen-marvel," declared by a "Chinese expert" (brought in especially to survey the newly appeared mass of moss) to be nothing other than a convention of frogs. "The police flew over the area in a helicopter, ascertaining that two hundred and seventy meters of road were covered with frogs so closely packed that they resembled a glistening carpet of moss" (35-36).

But more pertinent to this fine political novel, the "shadows" of the title represent a wholly negative feature of South American political reality: the "disappeared ones," whose mothers never give up hope of finding them alive but who return only as specters to haunt the oppressive and brutal world of the dictators. Thus the female protagonist of the work—who comes to realize that "until now I have been living a dream, and I'm afraid to wake up" (142)—undergoes a transformation: "Her nights were filled with fear: in her dreams she saw the ashen bodies in the morgue; [a friend] dangling like some grotesque fruit from a tree in the children's park; the endless lines of women inquiring about their *desaparecidos*" (152).[16] Likewise, the dream world of magical realism undergoes a transformation that results in a nightmare world of waking reality. "At times, the impression of nightmare was so strong that she was not sure whether she was alive dreaming, or dreaming she was alive" (285).

Woven within the bright, humorous side of the carnivalesque, with its convention of frogs, is the heroine's visit to the morgue and her first gruesome encounter with life's "other reality": "She could not absorb this hellish vision, and not even her wildest imagination could have measured the extent of such horrors. . . . She had never seen a dead body until the day she saw enough to fill her worst nightmares. She stopped before a large refrigerated cellar to look at a light-haired girl hanging on a meat hook in a row of bodies. . . . Horrified, she stared at the extensive beatings on the body, the burned face, the amputated hands" (116-18). Such images, with accompanying tortured realizations, one more likely expects to find in the literature of the Holocaust than in Latin American literature, acclaimed for its magical realism. But this is a work in which death by torture, execution, and suicide in the face of an uncompromising reality are likewise meant to be taken as commonplace.

> The extraordinary had come to seem natural, and he even found a certain logic in the situation; it was as if the violence had been there forever, waiting for him. Those dead bodies bursting from the earth, with fleshless hands and bullet holes in their skulls, had waited a long time ceaselessly calling to him, but it was only now he had ears to hear. He found himself talking aloud, apologizing for his delay, feeling that he had failed in the rendezvous. [A] voice calling from outside the mine brought him back to reality. He left part of his soul behind. [214]

In terms that are, paradoxically, distinctly magical realist and yet also wholly appropriate to such an intrusion of the horrific into the world of supposed magic, we are told in Gárcia Márquez' *Chronicle of a Death Foretold* (1981): "He was healthier than the rest of us, but when you listened with the stethoscope you could hear the tears bubbling inside his heart" (1984:41). There are like tears of remorse and anger amassing within the young journalists of Allende's novel, who find themselves confronting the gruesome remains of a dictator's secret police killers.

While the depiction of the dead engaging the living can be interpreted as a pronounced feature of the carnivalesque, in which the boundaries between the quick and the dead are at times erased, the "ceaseless calling" (just cited) is altogether dire and bleak, emphasizing twentieth-century atrocity rather than an atavistic echo of Menippean satire. In "a tomb filled with corpses, [where] parts of bodies [had] erupted from the earth" (Allende 1988:213), the awful revelation of so many dead ("who were beginning to spring out of the ground like weeds" 210) elicits the formation of a commission to investigate the awful matter. Amidst the human debris there appears a veritable "Vesuvius of piled up bones, hair and tattered cloth. Every stone they removed revealed new human remains" (225). The discovery bears a limited analogy to the findings of the liberators of the concentration camps at the end of the Second World War. But the atrocities here revealed (on a lesser scale) are also essentially inconceivable. Large numbers remain ciphers, a matter for statistics. We, as it is, can better absorb atrocity and death through a single telling instance.[17]

Gárcia Márquez implicitly makes the point in *Chronicle of a Death Foretold,* which takes as its subject a single instance of murder. In this tightly focused novella, the reader is told: "You can't imagine how hard it is to kill a man" (1984:140-41).[18] Yet, by showing unflinchingly the awful detail of just one killing, the most highly acclaimed writer of magical realism takes the event from the realm of the abstract and places it squarely in the real. ("Desperate, [he] gave him a horizontal slash on the stomach, and all his intestines exploded out." 141) Statistics, of course, can never achieve the effect of individuation. Gárcia Márquez' novella is magical realist but also horrific. In this tale of evisceration, we learn not only how much trouble the killed man's guts cause himself, as he staggers through the kitchen where he had received sustenance all his life ("They were sitting down to breakfast when they saw Santiago Nasar enter, soaked in blood and carrying the roots of his entrails in his hands" 142), but also how much difficulty they cause the village priest in his effort to do his sacred duty. "Furthermore, the priest had pulled out the sliced-up intestines by the roots, but in the end he didn't know what to do with them, and he gave them an angry blessing and threw them into the garbage pail" (88).

The whole town knows that one of its young men will be murdered that morning, yet no one attempts to alter the course of what is perceived as the workings of destiny, a code of honor, or the interaction of the two. (The result of the time-honored code demanding vengeance for a sister's honor is, in fact, twice graphically detailed: first, in the gruesome account of the knife wounds inflicted, as revealed by the autopsy; second, in the description of the repeated stabbing depicted at the end.) Seemingly, every individual in the town, including the destined victim, had been curiously indifferent to the impending doom, although "there had never been a death more foretold" (57). A like attitude, monumentally magnified, is repeatedly noted in the literature of the Holocaust that charts the indifference of virtually entire populations, which ignored for years the mass deportations and transports of innocent souls to their deaths.

Alejo Carpentier's *The Chase* (1956) also depicts the killing of a single individual. But in this complex novella the horrific is politicized, as the entire ploy turns on the carnivalesque premise and promise that fortune and destiny be reversed. In this case, the hunter becomes the hunted, the victimizer a victim, and the assassin yet another of the assassinated. But it all evolves slowly: "That same afternoon . . . he found protection just in time behind a column and saved himself from a barrage of bullets fired from a black car whose license plates were covered by a tangle of streamers. After all, it was carnival time" (1990:99). In the modern age, "carnival time" heralds a new and very different era from any bright semblance of carnival in the past. "It was a time when death sentences were passed from afar, a time for modest valor, a time for putting your life on the line. It was a time for dazzling executions carried out by an emissary wearing an implacable smile. . . . [a time when] exasperation unleashed terror in broad daylight" (82, 89). This is different from the killing in broad daylight that is depicted in Gárcia Márquez' novella. That murder, ultimately, can be explained away (and is by virtually everyone in the town) as the workings of an affair of honor which, traditionally, must take its course. ("We killed him openly . . . but we're innocent." 1984:55) In *The Chase,* with its overt political overtones, there is no question of a code of honor. This is simply the workings of a political force bent on maintaining power by means of whatever brutality is necessary.

In the carnivalesque twist of this work, the executioner is himself marked for death. Just as there was no other recourse for his victims, except to submit, now there is none for him. Oddly, the hopes of the former assassin are based on a like false hope for salvation that may have been shared by many of those herded onto the transports that hurtled through a ravaged Europe half a century ago: "I'm surrounded by people, protected by their bodies, hidden among their bodies; my body mixed in with many bodies; I've got to stay surrounded by their bodies" (Carpentier 1990:15).[19] But that wasted effort proves fruitless, of course, as does his belated reliance on the church. "Why didn't men today have that ancient option of 'claiming sanctuary.'. . . Oh, Jesus! If at least your Houses were open on this unending night so I could fall down on their paving stones in the peace of the naves, and groan and free myself of all that I have hidden in my heart!" (100). Now, in the grip of the same nauseating fear he himself had inspired in others, there is sounded (along with that plaint seeking the revival of a more humane, Christian past) a twin nostalgia, portentous and ominous, for the carnival-like atmosphere of pagan times. "We should go back to human sacrifice . . . to the teocali, where the priest squeezes out the fresh, juicy heart before tossing it onto a rotting pile of hearts; we should go back to the sacred horror of ritual immolations, to the flint knife that penetrates the flesh and slices open the rib cage. . . . We belong to this world . . . and we must return to our earliest traditions. We need chiefs and sacrificial priests, eagle warriors and leopard warriors; people like you" (108). That is, people who kill. Acknowledging, on the one hand, the indigenous roots of Latin America's past, such wistful longing also articulates the dream of the modern-day assassin eager to return to the most brutal practices of an earlier age. Yet, in such thinking, we also find the cruel indifference and self-deluding rationalizations that we might have thought belonged exclusively to the "bureaucracy of horror" (95) that had been instituted by the dictators of Europe: " 'It had to be done,' they [modern day political assassins] all say, their consciences in dialogue, looking for themselves in History. And they disperse into the night, without having to hide any longer or to distrust the shadows, because times have changed, repeating in louder and louder tones that *it* had been necessary so that we could be pure as we enter into the times that have changed" (87). According to just such specious argument, of course, has political expedience ("termination with extreme prejudice") been endlessly justified.

That solitary reference in *The Chase* to the "bureaucracy of horror," acknowledging Latin America's own creation of a full- blown twentieth-century apparatus for maiming and killing, finds its greater development in *Eva Luna,* where such a (generic) phrase is aptly extended and applied to the Europe of the dictators. In this novel, two stories are told alternately, the primary account relating the life of the novel's story-telling heroine, with the secondary tale devoted to a young Austrian immigrant to South America. In the second, parallel story of the novel, the reader is informed: "also in Europe reality took on abnormal dimensions. The war sank the world into confusion and fear. . . . Meanwhile, on this side of the ocean, few lost any sleep over that distant violence. They were sufficiently occupied with violence of their own" (Allende 1989:29). Relevant to our topic on several counts, these words acknowledge a concomitant European reality that is also extraordinary, although "abnormal" in an entirely different sense from that reality presented (at much greater length) in the primary story of the novel as magical realist. Still, an abnormal *European* reality plays a small but significant role in this Latin American tale of two lives that inevitably become interwoven.

Magical Realism

In effect, for some few pages of the novel (30-34), the literature of the Holocaust, an otherwise separate—but perhaps not entirely alien—genre, finds its place in a work exemplifying magical realism. Among the questions that have been raised here in this regard is the possible relation of the one form to the other. While that relation clearly exists, as has been shown, it is distinctly evident in *Eva Luna,* where the image of the Janus face, which figured so prominently earlier in this discussion, emerges once again clearly delineated: as the dark side of the human predilection to reverse traditional cultural values exists side by side with its corresponding brighter inclination. In this novel, a point of tangency between the two literary forms under consideration is established by the very fact that *Eva Luna* incorporates within its pages the horror of the concentration camp, as a frightening contrastive reality, in a book that nonetheless acknowledges an indigenous Latin American violence that must also be reckoned with (and reckoned with first).[20]

It is intimated that the young Austrian's father was himself a small cog in the Nazi torture machine and that his death by hanging at the hands of his former students (who knock the man unconscious with a rock and then hang him in a forest) was deserved on that and other counts. No reason is given for the murder other than the commonly held opinion that "[he] deserved it; he was a beast, a psychopath" (82). The novel succinctly gets at the core of Fascist thinking with the father's idea that "human beings are divided into anvils and hammers: some are born to beat, others to be beaten" (38). In this book, the Red Army plays a role, which is remarkable for the genre, as is the inclusion of the concentration camp dead ("There were dozens of them piled on the ground, one on top of another, a tangled, dismembered mass, a mountain of pale firewood. . . . [which] looked like the marionettes of some macabre theater"), a fact that inspires shame in the young Austrian, which "like a relentless nightmare would pursue him throughout his lifetime" (32-33).

A principal issue and concern of Holocaust writing is to reveal a world gone mad (not crazy), where unspeakable cruelty and abomination govern. On this side of the Janus face, cries, rather than laughter, predominate. To "speak" that cruelty, to bear witness, so that no one ever need bear such witness again, is the principal goal of this literary form. Yet, within the pages of *Eva Luna,* tellingly and eloquently, witness is borne to brutality and atrocity, since torture and terror are themselves not alien elements in the world of magical realism. Eva Luna is herself tortured to confess to a murder that never took place, while numerous references are made in the novel to maiming and killing as common events endemic to Latin American dictatorship. After all, as the novel recognizes, if torture and murder are condoned, it is but a short step, we may suppose, to mass extermination.

That short step is taken not only in Europe but also in Latin America, as is shown most graphically within Allende's *oeuvre* in *The House of the Spirits* (1982), where the magical realism of the first part of the book yields—in accord with that segment of twentieth-century history which the novel models—to the grotesque realism of the latter part, chronicling wide-scale torture and murder (in the author's native country of Chile). Hence the following passage, which might appear to have been drawn from the darkest pages of grotesque realism, nonetheless belongs to some of the finest writing of magical realism.

> They held him down by the arms. The first blow was to his stomach. After that they picked him up and smashed

Magical Realism

him down on a table. He felt them remove his clothes. . . . There wēre other prisoners in the same condition. They tied their hands and feet with barbed wire and threw them on their faces in the stalls. There [they] spent two days without food or water, rotting in their own excrement, blood, and fear. . . . In an empty lot they were shot on the ground, because they could no longer stand, and then their bodies were dynamited. The shock of the explosion and the stench of the remains floated in the air for a long time. [Allende 1986:371]

Further, in the kind of testament that is reminiscent of writers of the Holocaust, and that correlates with our own Janus face conception of carnival, Allende's heroine is advised to "write a testimony that might one day call attention to the terrible secret she was living through, so that the world would know about this horror that was taking place parallel to the peaceful existence of those who did not want to know, who could afford the illusion of a normal life . . . ignoring, despite all evidence, that only blocks away from their happy world there were others, these others who live or die on the dark side" (414). It is to that dark side, in its fuller development, that we turn now.

4 / GROTESQUE REALISM

> *It is possible that God exists, but at this point in history, with everything that has happened to us, does it matter?*
> —Mario Vargas Llosa [1991:92]

> *What can God tell us in our day and age?*
> —Yoram Kaniuk [1972:104]

Vargas Llosa's *The Storyteller* tells of an indigenous Peruvian tribe that periodically picks up its meager belongings and begins to migrate, with no special destination or goal, other than to prevent the sun from falling from the sky. In Appelfeld's *To the Land of the Cattails,* a woman makes her way home, after many travails, only to be shipped off immediately on a transport to the concentration camps and death. Perhaps the road and its mystique are all that these two works have in common.[1] However, the motif of the road plays a significant role in the literary representation of carnival, since, as Bakhtin notes, "the special Gogolian perception of 'the road' . . . has a purely carnival nature" (1968:289). Although being able to appreciate that "special Gogolian perception" depends largely on one's familiarity with Gogol's great comic work *Dead Souls* (1842), Bakhtin's observation holds true, even when divorced from Gogol, with regard to the affinity shared by the mystique of the road and the special "nature" of carnival. Only at times, that nature is manifested in dark, forbidding ways that Bakhtin himself may not have conceived.

Bakhtin sees in *Dead Souls* "a gay (carnivalesque) journey through the netherworld, through the land of death. . . . The world of *Dead Souls* is a world of gay nether regions. . . . In it we find the rabble and trash of the *carnival* hell" (1974:288). If appropriated by the collective endeavor to chart the effects of the war in literary form, particularly as experienced by its most persecuted genocide victims, Bakhtin's apt expressions concerning Gogol would appear hideously weak and insensitive; there would be no convenient way to justify the notion of a "gay . . . journey" or to provide a satisfactory analogy with the twin notions of a relatively innocuous "netherworld" or "gay nether regions." Bakhtin's references to "the land of death" and to "carnival hell," however, are indeed appropriate to the overall concerns of this study and especially the present chapter.

Yet what Bakhtin calls "a carnival sense of the world" is characterized definitively, in his view, by "an atmosphere of *joyful relativity*" (1984:107). This understanding originates in the Russian thinker's exploration of the past and in his attempt to explicate the sources of "that branch of artistic prose gravitating toward the novel and developing under its influence" (109). Hence, the nominal course of Bakhtin's thinking might appear to be past oriented, although the true thrust of his arguments is directed toward the modern period (Dostoevsky and beyond). Nevertheless, his appreciation for the basically innocuous concept of "joyful relativity" and the related idea (governing his thought) that affirms "dialogic means of seeking truth" (110) do not even remotely accommodate the literature evoked by the Holocaust, reflecting, as it does, a world doomed to the most hideous incarnation of monologic thought. So, as one of the conceptual bases of this book, Bakhtin's essentially positive view must be forgone in the present context in favor of a more neutral consideration of carnival, expressed simply by Jung as a "reversal of the hierarchic order" (1959:255), which, in this admittedly bland formulation, may nonetheless be conceived to include that profound contemporary narrative form that attempts to account for the experience of the Second World War.

In an incongruously understated formulation of the times, whose cruelty extends beyond what might otherwise still be called the *human* imagination, we read: "Of course, that was in the old days, the days of normal people.... This was nowadays, the days of madmen" (Fuks 1969:125). Or one might say, risking the charge of poor taste and gross insensitivity (no matter how strongly the case is put), that those were the days of the darkest (yet known to man) *carnivalized reality,* during which every "inconceivable" reproach to humanistic principle, humane conduct, and human dignity was, indeed, not only conceived but perpetrated.

> Beasts like the Nazis would find incredible things to do. He had heard that in concentration camps people were shut up in cells without windows and left to die of suffocation.
> Yet there could certainly be even worse things than suffocation for want of air. They could turn gas on in cells like that for they were indeed beasts who would think of things no normal person would do. [199-200]

So go the tortured ruminations and speculations of the gentle and naive Mr. Theodore Mundstock, one of the condemned.

To account for even the barest lineaments affording a poetics of grotesque realism, we need note, initially, the victims' haunting oppressive knowledge of being hunted; the fact that death is ever-present and continuously threatening; and that the time is Apocalypse, the end of time, when the gaping, sinister maw of hell opens to swallow a world of innocents en masse. "From now on there would be no difference, either in place or time. . . . here or in some other place, it made no difference" (Appelfeld 1980:85). Now there would be only one place, named Hell, and all, without further discrimination, would be its residents. The hopeful thinking of a deportee only highlights the underlying irony: "This is only a transition. Soon we'll arrive in Poland. . . . It's only a transition, only a transition" (143)—from the potential of carnival heaven to the absolute reality of carnival hell ("Heaven and hell merged into one" Appelfeld 1983:116), from life to death.

In Aharon Appelfeld's work, grim dramatic irony consistently plays a subdued role. In *The Retreat* (1984), a group of Jewish has-beens and ne'er-do-wells have gathered at a mountain retreat, presumably to undertake a regime of physical exercise designed to make them fit. Few actually undertake the program, which is just as well, since it has already been determined in the valley below that they are collectively unfit to live. Yet, collectively, this same people has its own way of looking at things, as is made evident in *Badenheim 1939* (1980), where attention to music still holds sway: "If the rumor that we're being transferred to Poland is right, we'll have to start studying. I don't know anything" (1980:73). "You wouldn't want us to appear in Poland unrehearsed, would you? What would people say?" (88). Ironically, the cultural, age-old reliance on education and study is once again

Grotesque Realism 107

intoned—but this time inappropriately and ineffectually—as a time-honored, proven resolution to virtually all ills and deprivations, except the one ill these forlorn figures must face: the impending deprivation of life. Hence the desperate poignancy attached to the stalwart remark: "We'll have to get used to the new way of life" (138). Which is certain death. Thus, the ultimate irony, the question of "what was going to happen in Poland" is answered: "It will be completely different. . . . You can't imagine how different it will be" (89-90). Those words, intended to be comforting, are unintentionally prophetic in literally the most "unimaginable" way. As D.M. Thomas suggests in *The White Hotel*: "There are things so far beyond belief that it ought to be possible to awake from them" (1982:288). Yet there is no awakening from the nightmare documented in this peculiarly twentieth-century brand of realism.

At the close of *The Retreat,* the daily routine of descending the mountain for supplies results in regular beatings, heralding worse things to come, administered to "inferior beings" who, in turn, do their best to provide first aid and succor to those who have been hurt. In the book's characteristically understated concluding lines, we learn that, "At night, of course, people were afraid. But they helped one another. If a man fell or was beaten he was not abandoned" (Appelfeld 1984:164). Similarly, in *Badenheim 1939,* confronted with deportation and gross uncertainty, a lone figure packs up the residents of his aquarium to travel with him in a bottle, in a desperate attempt to provide caring and life in an atmosphere of horrific neglect and death. Another deportee is equally concerned to preserve the town's sorry mongrel population. However, in response to the starkly contrastive distinction between caring victim and determined tormentor, there is ever present, as Wiesel points out, the self-serving rationale declaring that "the killer knows that he is following the right way. 'We're doing it for the good of mankind,' [claims] the philosopher of murder, waiting for the rest of the world to congratulate them" (1967:68). Although the expected congratulations may never be forthcoming, this all too common justification of gross persecution has nonetheless never been wanting. Moreover, if it were needed to make a case for the possible existence of an archetypal notion that argues for a great chain of being, in which one people is situated higher on an invidiously hypothesized ladder of human development than another, one might consult *The Lost Steps,* an intriguing literary documentary (if not a "valid" anthropological sourcebook), which provides a case in point, as a primitive Indian tribe is shown holding "inferior beings" in a jungle prison. In *The Retreat,* the only difference is that "lowlier" souls are in effect imprisoned on a mountain top. Otherwise, the principle is sadly the same.

Arguably the most poignant irony of a genre documenting the disappearance of whole populations is that the victims were able perhaps only in nightmare, or in death ("The dead slept, and in their dreams they saw the ditches filling without end" Wiesel 1967:159), to conceive the dread fate that awaited them. Otherwise, it might all have appeared utterly innocuous and banal.

> An engine, an engine coupled to four filthy freight cars, emerged from the hills and stopped at the station. Its appearance was as sudden as if it had risen from a pit in the ground [or from Hell]. . . . And the people were sucked in. Even those who were standing with a bottle of lemonade in their hands, a bar of chocolate, the headwaiter with his dog—they were all sucked in as easily

as grains of wheat poured into a funnel. [Appelfeld 1980:147-48]

That metaphor, stunning in its simplicity, coupled with the "reduction" of humanity to a small cast of characters whose size accommodates human comprehension, shows, simply and terribly, how it happened, over and over again, to millions of people.

In Appelfeld's works, the Jew appears a peculiar figure, strange and estranged, an anomaly in both speech and manner. He is the eternal, unenviable outsider who participates only marginally in the physical aspect of life. Unprepossessing, he is shown nonetheless as utterly human in his frailty, in the need to understand and consequent invention of varied and numerous rationalizations to explain his mysterious, hideous plight. Hence one lonely figure's strained explanation for their mass deportation: "In the last analysis, a man has to return to his origins" (89). That dubious philosophical view is later capped by the novel's ironic last line, meant to ameliorate for others, as much as for the speaker, the shock of the miserable freight train used for their transport: "If the coaches are so dirty it must mean that we have not far to go" (148).

In seeking to elaborate further a poetics of grotesque realism, we must look to representative instances of allegorical imagery and unusual metaphor, as well as to analogies made to the animal world, where predator and victim are tellingly portrayed.

> A nature lover had brought some Cambium fishes and persuaded the hotel owner to put them in with the other fish. The hotel owner was a little apprehensive about these blue fish, but in the end he agreed. For the first

few days the blue Cambium fish deported themselves gaily in the water, but one night they suddenly fell on the other fish and massacred them horribly. In the morning the floor of the aquarium was full of corpses. [Appelfeld 1980:51]

"The fish in the aquarium, what's happened to the fish in the aquarium?"
"Nothing, they're swimming as usual."
"I mean the green ones; where have the green ones disappeared to?"
"How strange.... You watch them all the time."
"The green ones, the prettiest fish in the aquarium, have disappeared without anyone even noticing." [57]

In a few sparse, fugitive instances, the world of the aquarium is likened to the domain of man, as the blue predators destroy their "pretty" green victims, while a condemning inattention and lack of concern extends to indifferent spectators everywhere.

A more proliferated and more extreme use of animal imagery permeates *The Painted Bird,* Jerzy Kosinski's masterwork of horror and despair at the human capacity (or, better, ingenuity) for devising acts of cruelty, principally against one's fellow human being. In a telling instance that focuses upon the animal world—but that resonates in the world of man—a rabbit is literally (although mistakenly) skinned alive. "The partially skinned carcass started to jump and squirm on the post where it was suspended.... The struggling rabbit ... fell down and started running immediately, now forward, now backward. With her skin hanging down behind her.... she lost all sense of direction, blinded by flaps of skin falling over her eyes, catching twigs and weeds with it as with a half pulled-off stocking." The reaction of the other creatures in the yard corresponds tellingly with the similarly awful human condition. "Her piercing shrieks caused pandemonium in the yard. The terrified rabbits went mad in their hutches, the excited females trampled their young, the males fought one another, squealing.... The hens flapped their wings in a desperate attempt to fly away from it all and then collapsed, resigned and humiliated" (1966:133)—as had all those caged up in the railroad cars and crammed into bunks in the camps, who also lived in terror of the awful fate that awaited them.

The title of Kosinski's powerful novel serves to register its governing metaphor. In a small allegorical account, a tale among many strung together, giving structure to the work as a whole, a peasant displays his perverted appreciation for birds by catching and painting them, then sending them off to join their own kind—which invariably reject and then kill them. In relating the disturbing adventures of a dark-haired, dark-eyed boy in an alien world of blond hair and light eyes, the novel presents a modern-day parable: once the birds are painted, they appear different from the others and are therefore killed. Is this some horrible law of nature, or an archetypal pattern? Are all those creatures who are somehow different condemned a priori on appearance alone? In this journey of a child through a twentieth-century, manmade hell, the implicit response is unequivocally affirmative.

The novel depicts the world of the East European peasant—backward, ignorant, superstitious, and unconscionably cruel. The mind and intellect of this figure, seemingly concocted from a veritable witch's brew, is haunted by the ever-present threat of the plague and ignominious death. This is the nightmare world of the Second World War, which is here juxtaposed to the relatively dreamy magical realism of Latin America, where violence finds a peaceful and joyous counterpart, coupled with at least the possibility of resurrection from evil or villainy, a potentiality that is absent from grotesque realism. In this literary mode, when a child is tossed into a stream to float away (and presumably drown) on the bloated bladder of a monstrous catfish (Kosinski 1966:22-23), the reader—rather than seek a wondrous (magical) source of possible rejuvenation—is thrust squarely into the realm of nightmare, the peculiar domain of man, which remains untamed and unrestrained by any likelihood or even conception of a higher ideal.

In this world, God is relegated to the periphery of things. To be sure, there are priests, catechisms, and prayers that are said. But all of that skates across the surface of the text, principally, as irony. On the one hand, there is the felicitous fact that, when hung by his wrists for hours by a brutal peasant (whose dog thirsts for blood below), the boy manages to overcome the pain and exhaustion, and to survive by repeating prayers that he has learned by rote, does not understand, but thinks can help. ("Thus my life was spent alternately praying and being beaten." 113) In fact, they do help, since they provide a necessary and welcome distraction ("When I hung on my straps I concentrated on my prayers to the exclusion of all else" 118), as well as a penetrating insight into the psychology of the survivor, who is able (even as a child) to endure by concentrating on something other than his pain. But the prayers also afford a telling irony, for in all the ritualistic "worship" and endless prayer recitals, practiced by the boy as well as the peasants, there is absolutely nothing of Spirit, of a truly religious understanding of faith, or belief in God. Rather, prayer is just another form of peasant superstition, akin to counting the teeth of one's enemy, whenever possible, in order to establish and maintain power over him.[2]

Of paramount importance in our effort to delineate a poetics of the genre, *The Painted Bird,* a quintessential work of grotesque realism, is first of all about survival. No matter how terrifying the adventures recounted in that novel or in related works, nothing less than survival is ultimately and always what is at stake. Either the story of the war is an account of survival against harrowing odds or it is the more common tale of destruction and obliteration. Survival, when it does occur, is always at a price that is excruciatingly high, whether it is that of Appelfeld's "immortal Bartfuss," who survives as a legend among survivors but has lost the ability to feel, or Wiesel's "little prince," a boy who survives the camps but whose childhood has been consigned to the flames. When he bemoans his fate—"I'm not a child, and can't be one" (1969:72)—he does so in terms that hold equally true for the protagonist of *The Painted Bird*. Not for a moment can the boy in Kosinski's harrowing, twentieth-century "picaresque" relax his guard or think of anything other than how to survive, as he proceeds (in what amounts to a horrific "pilgrim's progress") from one frightening, calamitous situation to another in a man-centered universe where God is either notably absent or, at best, only vaguely present, somewhere on the periphery of human existence.

But to use the word "human" in the context of the world into which the boy is thrust (by his parents in the hope that he might survive) raises problems of its own. Is the peasant who repeatedly beats and tortures an innocent child (to say "for no reason" seems absurdly superfluous) human? Is there anything human in the nature of this manmade, wartorn, spiritually and physically ravaged place that was Eastern Europe half a century ago? The irony expressed in that question is far more profound than the fact that the boy manages to save himself through the mindless repetition of quasi-religious, superstitious phrases. Reduced to another level of paradox, a related question asks: Is there any humanity in human beings? Or, posed in Ivan Karamazov's terms: If man is created in God's image, then how do we account for the child torturer? If this is God's creation, then how can these terrible things be allowed to happen? That is the fundamental question, the ultimate paradox, upon which the genre is based. Regardless of the supposed existential stance of the author, or whether God's existence is taken into account (as in Wiesel's writings), or ignored (as in Appelfeld's), the implicit query nonetheless remains present in the mind of the reader (whether literally for the believer or symbolically for the atheist): "Where was He all these years?" (Kaniuk 1972:74).

In Kosinski's novel, we sense that all of the events related indeed happened—but whether to the boy who is at the center of it all, as the consciousness through which everything is filtered, remains basically irrelevant—because the book yields an uncanny feel for truth. Everything documented—and worse—did happen. The novel affords an extraordinary sense of the terror produced by the war in Nazi-dominated Europe, where crimes against humanity were perpetrated repeatedly under the guiding spirit of fascism—which states in one form or another that, if you have dark hair and dark eyes and I have blond hair and blue eyes, then I have the right to kill you. That is what the boy must struggle against. He is born into a world permeated with hatred, which he constantly tries to understand—but always to no avail. Neither the superstitious practices of the peasantry nor the pious sayings of the priests help the struggling boy to comprehend what is at base evil.

The book shows through terrible event and fearful imagery a single, perhaps primary, sin: ignorance. The peasants are of course unschooled; but they are also ignorant—perversely so—of the pain they cause others, willingly, happily, *laughingly*. Repeatedly, throughout the book, the "folk" stand

Grotesque Realism

by and laugh at another's pain, grief, or death. Conceivably their grotesque laughter (at the brutal, disgusting killing of a mad woman; at the boy's endless torments) is what makes them, seemingly, less than human. Needless to say, it is precisely such ignorance—perverse, brutal, and cruel—that allows fascism to thrive in the first place. But our topic is the carnivalesque(-grotesque), and perhaps nowhere in this wide-ranging literary investigation do we find the dark side of that impulse, attitude, or "spirit" so well illustrated as being deleterious and dangerous, as in Kosinski's novel, which treats so incisively this single aspect of what Bakhtin refers to—from a far brighter vantage point—as folk culture.

The Painted Bird is episodic and essentially plotless. It is structured according to the earliest novelistic design, as a picaresque, in which the hero makes his way, however he can, through the countryside and a series of strange adventures that are inherent to the genre, the road, and the rogue, who traipses within and along the one and the other. In this genre, one event simply and necessarily leads to the next, with no attendant psychological or compositional complexities. In effect, the work is structured as a kind of square dance, as one partner takes hold of the hero and sends him in one direction, where he locks arms with another, and goes off a different way. Only in this work, and this genre, the dance is a *danse macabre*—a dance of torture and death ("A striptease of torture. Stripping, stripping, trampling, smashing" Kaniuk 1972:35),[3] where the novelist borrows features from the earliest form of the novel to depict what the earliest practitioners of that form could never have imagined. What God, perhaps, might not have imagined.

Part of what makes *The Painted Bird* a remarkable work is the fact that it draws upon detail that, in another literary context, would likely be regarded as magical realist. A quintessential work of grotesque realism, perhaps even *the* definitive work of the genre, the book also serves as bridge to the realm of magical realism. In an early descriptive passage, the reader is told: "Her long hair, never combed, had knotted itself into innumerable thick braids impossible to unravel. These she called elflocks. Evil forces nested in the elflocks, twisting them and slowly inducing senility" (1966:3). This information, with the characteristic insistence of the genre upon *evil* forces at work is related as absolute fact. For the boy to absorb it as such is understandable, since his mind represents a clear-cut instance of a tabula rasa. But those much older with whom he comes into contact also regard the world with the kind of certainty that is derived from legend and tale, folk wisdom and folk folly. Thus, when the boy sees a snake discard its skin, he is informed that "the human soul discards the body in a similar manner and then flies up to God's feet. After its long journey God picks it up in his warm hands, revives it with His breath, and then either turns it into a heavenly angel or casts it down into hell for eternal torture by fire" (5). The boy turns out to be a good learner, and is soon both seeing things on his own and figuring things out for himself.

> Phantoms drifted around me. A phantom . . . trips people in fields and forests, peeks into huts, can turn itself into a vicious cat or rabid dog. . . . At midnight it turns into hot tar.
> Ghosts . . . are persons long dead, condemned to eternal damnation, returning to life only at full moon.
> Vampires are people who were drowned without having first been baptized or who were abandoned by their mothers. They . . . maliciously soil the pictures of the saints, bite, break, or destroy the holy objects and, when possible, suck blood from sleeping men. [17]

Grotesque Realism 117

> I saw witches hanging from the trees. They stared at me, trying to lead me astray and confuse me. I distinctly heard the shudders of wandering souls which had escaped from the bodies of penitent sinners. [28]

Such explanations (and visions) belong, of course, to the people. Their beliefs and superstitions, as ways of explaining peculiar, even imaginary manifestations are a source of both magical and grotesque realism. The former is replete with such sagacity.

> Even happiness gets tired after a while. . . . Every time you sigh, a little bit of your life goes out of you. [Rulfo 1969:40-41]

> Some villages taste of bad luck. You can tell them by drinking a little of their stale air. It's poor and thin, like everything else that's old. [81]

> Broth made from young condor fights madness and frees up your dreams. [Fuentes 1992:78]

> The only cure for asthma is the prolonged embrace of a loved one. [Allende 1986:282]

> A person does not belong to a place until there is someone dead under the ground. [Gárcia Márquez 1971:22]

> Children inherit their parents' madness. [46]

Derived from essentially the same generic source, a related vision of things is equally common to *The Painted Bird*. In part, that source represents in this novel a peculiar blend of folk wisdom filtered through the mind of an impressionable boy. ("The plague subsided and fresh grass grew on the many new graves, grass that one could not touch because it surely contained poison from the plague victims." 22) In addition, the broth is greatly spiced by the inclusion of events that are truly horrific rather than "magic." The boy witnesses, for instance, a jealous miller put out the eyes of a handsome young man with a spoon. The boy is intrigued with the eyes, now freed forever from their sockets, "as though they had acquired a new life and motion of their own. I watched them with fascination.... Surely they could still see." A pair of cats plays with the eyes rolling on the floor, as fascinated as the boy, until the miller, angered still further, squashes them underfoot. "Something popped under his thick sole. A marvelous mirror, which could reflect the whole world, was broken. There remained on the floor only a crushed bit of jelly. I felt a terrible sense of loss" (34). On the one hand, in this grotesque passage, what is wondrous and "marvelous" in life is acknowledged, even at the moment of its very destruction. But, immediately following, and thoroughly typical of the genre, is a "terrible sense of loss." Clearly, the governing principle at work in this novel is the intermeshing of a child's tortured but still innocent point of view with the peasants' (his only teachers) understanding of phenomena. Those phenomena, however, presented for the child's explorations and perceptions of the world, are for the most part unutterably grotesque.

    Nonetheless, as previously noted, magical realism is born from the disparity between the child's original (still unscathed) point of view and the adult's. Within that literary practice, the challenge to the novelist is to reveal the child's perspective as vital and still functioning in the adult. In *The Painted Bird,* conversely, it is not so much the case that the child is never shown grown up as that the boy cannot remain a child in the world to which he has been condemned. He must absorb adult perceptions as quickly as he can in order to survive. In the Janus face construed from our twin genres, the magical side looks for the child in the adult, while the grotesque aspect necessarily seeks the adult in the child. Yet, it is still the same face, and therefore we can make essentially the same case: namely, that while the child's perspective can be summed up initially as a "blank slate," the corresponding point of view of the adult is animated principally by a reliance on folk wisdom—which, in both related genres, provides a vital source of (mis)understanding. In effect, magical realism and its grotesque counterpart borrow as much from the wisdom as from the folly of the "people"—that much touted abstraction, which Bakhtin refers to as the "protagonist of carnival" (1968:250). But what can we hope to learn from this erratic (collective) protagonist?

In this case, the protagonist is not only erratic but also "two-faced," masking folly behind its supposed wisdom. Regarding this masked feature (which may be the more interesting), Bakhtin observes: "Folly is . . . deeply ambivalent. It has the negative element of debasement and destruction . . . and the positive element of renewal and truth. Folly is the opposite of wisdom—inverted wisdom, inverted truth. It is the other side, the lower stratum of official laws and conventions, derived from them. Folly is a form of gay festive wisdom, free from all laws and restrictions, as well as from preoccupations and seriousness" (260). Conceived in another context, Bakhtin's perspective still largely accommodates our own. The ambivalence he underscores is entirely appropriate: we can laugh (in true carnival spirit) at the wisdom/folly of magical realism, but we shudder at its sometimes ghastly results in grotesque realism. Broadly speaking, the "negative element of debasement and destruction" also fits more closely with grotesque realism, while the "positive element of renewal" is more in accord with magical realism. Finally, that folly is "the opposite of wisdom—inverted wisdom" and (perhaps even closer to the mark in our dual context) "inverted truth" is very much to the point here: namely, that as a source of our twin genres, folk wisdom/folly produces mixed results, misperceptions, "understandings" that run contrary to all understanding, amidst conclusions that are either ludicrous or hideous, or mad.[4]

Both magical realism and grotesque realism are born not only from the ancient tale, legend, and myth but also from the darker aspect of folk "wisdom" that includes superstition and false belief. Thus, in *The Painted Bird,* we read: "It was said that Ludmilla lived with this huge dog as with a man. Others said that someday she would give birth to children whose bodies would be covered with canine hair and who would have lupine ears and four paws, and that these monsters would live somewhere in the forest" (Kosinski 1966:42). As a result of this kind of popular speculation, we might well imagine a corresponding *fiction* in which sightings of such strange creatures are commonplace. Yet, as a result of such "sightings," we might also presume the emergence of a new hybrid form or literary equivalent to magical realism—unless that "new" form has already made its appearance under the designation we have given it as grotesque realism.

What distinguishes grotesque realism from its "magical" counterpart is, as previously noted, its consistent emphasis upon "evil forces" operating to the virtual exclusion of a potential positive correlative. The nightmare vision of *The Painted Bird* is presented repeatedly through stark, frightening imagery—the burning of a peasant's hut with the seated corpse of an old woman inside, the boy set adrift on a bloated fish bladder to drown, a young man blinded with a spoon, cats' playing with plucked-out eyes, the night replete with both imagined and real horrors. Those horrors include the

Grotesque Realism 121

peasants themselves, who rape and kill, and who laugh when a woman they have repeatedly raped—leaving her mind unhinged—is later brutally murdered by the other women of the village in cruel revenge for being too "loose." Throughout this and other scenes of brutality the peasants' cruel laughter rings loud as a welcoming knell for the appearance of the more advanced, calculated cruelty of the Nazi torturer. Perhaps the most telling image in the book is that of rats at the bottom of a pit hastily devouring a man down to the bone (55-56). That image serves well as a hallmark picture of the Holocaust and how it likewise reduced millions to cleanly picked skeletons, or ash.

    The extent of the Nazi horror is dispassionately related when the peasants are shown indifferently observing the packed cattle cars crammed with human beings on their way to the crematoria. At best the villagers express only vague curiosity; no one cares. The blood drinkers of Christian babies are getting what they deserve. For the peasants (as we saw in *The White Hotel*), anyone managing to escape from the death trains is only a source of additional clothing and nothing more. Any hope on the part of the victims for human kindness or assistance is pointless. The boy who knows no other reality can only wonder: "Wouldn't it be easier to change people's eyes and hair than to build big furnaces and then catch Jews and Gypsies to burn in them? . . . I wondered whether so many Jews were necessary to compensate God for the killing of His son. Perhaps the world would soon become one vast incinerator for burning people" (88-89). Given the perspective the boy acquires on this house of horrors, which is the world, that conclusion is as reasonable as any.[5]

    When given the opportunity by his parents (who have managed to locate him) to escape the terror that has been his life, however, the boy does not wish to give up living on the edge, where life is a matter of survival, in return for the comforts of home. For him, there is barely the chance to return "home"—because he has not retained through the terror of the war years any sense of what home is, or might be. He longs for a world at war, for struggle, for life in extremis, for a world turned upside down—no matter how ugly the underside might be—for the world of carnival. "I was somehow disappointed; the war seemed to be over. . . . I would much prefer to be alone again, wandering from one village to the next, from one town to another, never knowing what might happen. Here everything was very predictable" (163, 208). Here life proceeded according to the rules of the "official culture," and what he longs for is "unofficial" and unlawful. So the boy chooses to live his life at night, since "in daytime the world was at peace. The war continued at night" (210). At night he can still have uncertainty, unpredictability, the war—and carnival.

Nowhere in the novel is war and carnival so horrifically intertwined as in the account of the wholesale raping, pillaging, and killing by the Kalmuks,[6] accomplished in all manner of ingenious ways, concluded only by the arrival of an avenging Red Army, which puts an end to the slaughter by initiating, in turn, a new round of killings. In the vicious grotesquerie, no one escapes: neither victim, nor victimizer. Here there is no shortage of victims or killers. A procession of the one is, seemingly, followed en masse by the other. Nor does the human imagination, evidently, want for ways to dehumanize, hurt, maim, and destroy, as just the opening lines of several successive paragraphs show.

> The Kalmuks were now dragging a half-naked woman out of a house. . . . Nearby the soldiers had forced a woman to the ground. . . . Still another woman was brought out. . . . The screams of raped women were

Grotesque Realism

heard in all the houses. . . . New victims were being caught all the time. . . . Other feats followed. Helpless women were passed from one trotting horse to another. One of the Kalmuks tried to couple with a mare. [158-60]

Thriving on the life blood of their victims one day, the killers are themselves made to suffer an excruciating death the next, when they are captured and left hanging upside down "from the oak trees along the river. . . . like sapless overgrown pine cones" (164)—"the landscape [having] become a phantasmagoria, with strange human fruit hanging from the [trees]" (Vargas Llosa 1985:287). "Ants and flies crawled all over the strung-up Kalmuks. They crept into their open mouths, into their noses and eyes. They set up nests in their ears; they swarmed over their ragged hair. They came in thousands and fought for the best spots" (Kosinski 1966:164-65). Yet this is only the twentieth-century version of the terrifically brutal history of Eastern Europe, where nothing changes, only time passes, as new players with more advanced methods of torture appear on the stage. As for the boy: "I looked around for death, for I felt its breath in the air. . . . It was nearer to me than ever. I could almost touch its airy shroud. . . . It stopped in front of me. . . . I was not afraid of it; I hoped it would take me along. . . . I reached out my hand, but death vanished among the trees with their burden of rustling leaves and heavy crop of hanging corpses" (165). Death would have been welcome. After all, who wants to grow up and live in a world such as the one—the only one—the boy has come to know?

The war years have no comparable period in world history. More than fifty million people died during those years. That kind of monumental figure has no counterpart, nor any real meaning for the human mind. Untold millions experienced terrible suffering, uprootedness, loss of family and friends, loss of a place in the world that had been familiar and comfortable. The world has seen nothing remotely like the devastation and desolation caused by the Second World War. Not surprisingly, this incomparable period has brought forth a new literature, which is still emerging with new shoots in what might otherwise have remained a barren place.

The Painted Bird is thus one among many works that explore a grossly negative psychology that in some way may be seen as a twentieth-century malady: a human being is made to suffer (in war, in prison, as a member of the underground living under great deprivation), but when the period of suffering is over, that person develops the need to recreate it, to reestablish some source of hurt in his life as a kind of supreme reality—perhaps the only reality—that he can understand.[7] The idea behind such awful possibility is that such an individual may no longer be able (or want) to live a normal life with all of its attendant minor hurts and pains. What is sought and needed, rather, is something large—and tremendously detrimental to life—that he can once again struggle to overcome. This is the psychology of a type that evolves from suffering—in war, in the Holocaust; it is a psychology that demands the extreme, that expresses the need to live on the very edge of life and meaning.

In Aharon Appelfeld's *The Immortal Bartfuss* (1988), we can only surmise that the hero survived the war and the Holocaust under extraordinary circumstances. We are given a hint of his remarkable survivalist abilities when a character suggests with hyperbolic awe reminiscent of the magical realist tendency to exaggerate possibility: "There are fifty bullets in his body. How can a man live with fifty bullets in his body?" (1989:62). That inexplicable "fact" is superseded, however, by a more pressing dilemma. According to Bartfuss'

Grotesque Realism

thinking: "People were born for solitude. Solitude was their only humanity" (100). That view bears directly on the question of man's place in the world: to be with others and enjoy the solicitude such company offers, or to remain in solitude as "one's only humanity." In dealing with such existential problems, the book rightly presents them as issues that are born *not* of philosophical speculation or concern for the human condition but from concrete historical reality. Bartfuss is a Holocaust survivor. That makes his human predicament all the more demanding: how does he square the fact that he survived when millions of others were killed? His concern goes beyond the age-old petulant question, Why was I born? to, Why was I saved? In his mind, the fact that he had been saved might suggest of itself that there had also been a reason for his being spared.[8]

The immediate challenge facing Bartfuss is to discover that reason. Others might wonder periodically why they have been placed on the planet; Bartfuss needs to know why he had not been obliterated from it when so many others were. For him—and this is an implicit point of the book—it is hard to remain alive when others are dead. For other survivors, he is a source of wonderment, a living legend ("They tell amazing stories about you. . . . They tell astounding things about you. . . . Let me touch you" 33). But Bartfuss is not a source of wonderment to himself and does not want to be at the center of others' idol worship. ("Bartfuss. It's Bartfuss. Haven't you heard about him?" 60) Now he is a man seemingly devoid of human sentiment. He does not want even a *word* for himself. "A word for yourself," is what he is told he needs, to which he responds: "I don't need words" (101). All Bartfuss knows for sure is: "I'm alive. . . . I'm alive again" (37-38). That is all he knows and all he can know. So the fact that he has survived must be sufficient; words, in this context, become unnecessary. But what kind of life is it to deprive oneself of the very possibility of human communication? That is one of the profound existential questions posed by this work.[9]

The existential quality of the book is rooted not in the story nor in the psychology of Bartfuss but in history. Hence the preponderant dilemma: "No one knew what to do with the lives that had been saved. The lives that had been saved strove for great deeds" (36). Evidently such deeds had been accomplished when life was still lived on the run, when Bartfuss "lived for the strong taste of action on others' behalf" (20). The reader never learns precisely what those actions were. We can only assume that there were "great deeds" that resulted in the saving of lives in the fight against fascism. But now in the relative comfort of the postwar years there is no heroism but only the ongoing petty war among family members, while Bartfuss ruminates: "I should have been more generous. People who went through the Holocaust should be generous. . . . I expect . . . greatness of soul from people who underwent the Holocaust" (73, 107).[10] But, needless to say, that amounts to a great expectation, whether of oneself or others.

Like the boy in *The Painted Bird,* Bartfuss has lost interest in everyday, mundane concerns. And, like the boy, who for a long period of time loses the ability to speak, Bartfuss may have lost the capacity to value the Word, to appreciate the human effort at trying to understand, and be understood by, one's fellow beings.[11] As a kind of perversity, born of a terrible adversity that few ever come to know, Bartfuss perceives others' speech as noise and therefore as something to be ignored or abhorred.[12] Yet part of what makes this novel important is the fact that the Word is made virtually equivalent to a character within the book. We learn how Bartfuss uses and reacts to words—his own and those of others—how other characters treat words as wholly significant objects in their lives. Paradoxically, the Word is made vital and alive by virtue of the main character rejecting it so vigorously, by effecting "the presence of an absence" (Fuentes 1992:142). In *Bartfuss,* through subtle literary artifice, the Word is made a thing and is thus treated as a material object. It is not taken for granted as the raw material of which this work—and all literature—is made. Rather, the reader's attention is constantly drawn to the Word as an entity that exists in its own right, as an existential fact of immense power and importance. For "all power is in words, in the sound of words" (Asturias 1982:118).

But why should we attribute so much power to words? Because, from one (spiritual) perspective, "in taking a single word by assault it is possible to discover the secret of creation, the center where all threads come together" (Wiesel 1967:168). And, from another like perspective, if "the secret of creation" is not yet to be revealed, we may still acknowledge that "the word is the only thing that links us when everything else becomes useless, treacherous, threatening. The word is the ultimate reality of Christ, His vigil among us, what allows us, without pride to say, 'I am like Him' " (Fuentes 1992:227). Hence, the Word may be perceived as Spirit, as the binding agent between man and man, and between man and God.

In the far distant context of medieval culture, Bakhtin refers to "virginal words" that "emerged from the depths of the people's elemental life and entered the system of written and printed literature" (1968:456). New forms figure in essentially the same sense in magical realist works, where expressions derived from the "elemental life," as well as from the legends and mythologies of the indigenous Latin American peoples, enter contemporary literature (*The Storyteller*).

The "virginal words" of grotesque realism, however, infiltrate their corresponding literary sphere in a parallel but ominous fashion, as neologisms ("kapo") and other new formulations ("final solution"; "night and fog"[13]) that horrify rather than edify. Further, Bakhtin observes that Rabelais had learned new words and expressions from an oral source that had never been used in a literary context (457-58). Essentially the same can be said concerning magical realism and grotesque realism. Both forms draw significantly from colloquial speech that had never existed in print before, in part to convey experiences or events, especially in the latter case, that had never been known before.[14]

In regarding the Word as an independent entity, *Bartfuss* explores the underside of dialogue: the potential tyranny of words. "She always rushed in to explain, to dispel, to pile words upon words. . . . Once her outbursts used to fill his entire day with noise. . . . Sometimes the married daughter bursts in with her mother's noise and lays down masses of words" (Appelfeld 1989:4, 8). The first few pages of this work thus insist upon the materiality of the Word—its mass. Later, "scraps of words" (12, 61) are brought to our attention, so that they become almost palpable in their (stinging) presence *and* absence: "They used to call him 'him.' 'He' was a stranger of whom one had to be wary" (11). In this way, "he" is deprived of a *name* and affection.[15] Paradoxically, the various negations of common verbal usage illustrated in this novel serve to underscore the creative potential inherent within the linguistic pool we all share: to elaborate a mode of speech that is either loving or distancing in its relation to others.

Yet "the all-encompassing power of words" (Allende 1989:297) is of course not a part of the exclusive provenance of Appelfeld or any other artist of the word. There is a like preoccupation with the Word and its evocatory power in magical realist texts as well. For instance, the trip through time in *The Lost Steps* leads Carpentier's hero to discover the origin of the Word ("And in the vast night jungle filling with night terrors, there arose the Word")—born as an incantation against death: "The earliest attempt to combat the forces of annihilation which frustrate man's designs" (1979:162-63). But those same designs can also be frustrated by a different interpretation placed on a word than the accepted connotation. Thus, in *Eva Luna,* striking differences of interpretation emerge between understandings of the terms "murdered" (which expresses the horror of the humanist) and "executed" (which conveys the political necessity perceived by the terrorist). Likewise, the young heroine's romantic perception of her friends as "guerrillas" is countered by the view of them by her admirer (a general) as "terrorists" (Allende 1989:231, 302).

Varying connotations are thus linked to various social and political positions and attendant perceptions. In *Of Love and Shadows,* we read: " 'Justice' was an almost forgotten term, no longer mentioned because, like the word 'liberty,' it had subversive overtones" (Allende 1988:214). Likewise, in *The House of the Spirits*: "There were words prohibited by military decree . . . and others that could not be mentioned even though no edict had swept them from the lexicon, such as 'freedom,' 'justice' " (Allende 1986:383). The converse of such repressive official reactions to the Word is expressed on the plane of the personal and individual in Appelfeld's *Badenheim 1939*: "The words *procedure* and *appeal* seemed to satisfy him. . . . He calmed down a little. The contact with the old words restored him to his sanity" (1980:99). Hence the potential healing power of familiar verbal signs. Yet that "restoration" is short-lived. For, in this instance, too, the humanist's understanding of legal or humane procedures does not jibe with (Nazi) officialdom's point of view, leaving the healing, restorative power of the Word, in this context, to fail in its seeking to give succor, to preserve human life.

Generally, less is at stake in the carnival attitude to the Word, by which commonly accepted verbal connotations may be subjected to various reversals or transformations. Accomplished through superimposing new layers of potential meaning upon the old, such reversals seek a corresponding new truth in seeming opposites. As Bakhtin puts it: "Thought and word were searching for a new reality beyond the visible horizon of official philosophy. Often enough words and thoughts were turned around in order to discover what they were actually hiding, what was that other side. The aim was to find a position permitting a look at the other side of established values, so that new bearings could be taken" (1968:272). Charted in such sober fashion is the often chaotic carnival spirit that seeks to oppose official positions with new unofficial viewpoints. Literature, by contrast, can of course dispense with the more temperate manner of expression of the cultural historian in documenting the resultant frictions between those who regard the Word with sympathy and those who do so with antipathy, between the received perception of its value as forever rooted in official terms and that of its creative potential realized and revitalized in unofficial carnivalized expression.

Thus, in a related classic opposition, we find mirrored in magical realism the thought of "civilized" man juxtaposed to that of his more "primitive" counterpart (a prominent theme of *The Lost Steps*), in whom there may be an even greater preoccupation with "wisdom," the seeking to understand nature and man's place within it, rather than in acquiring (scientific) knowledge. That preoccupation is well documented in *The Storyteller,* in which the indigenous people's concern with retaining, against great odds,

Grotesque Realism 131

the understanding acquired through generations is repeatedly noted:

> Who knows whether wisdom had yet appeared? [Vargas Llosa 1990:41]
>
> Wisdom was lost or hadn't yet come. [42]
>
> And wisdom returned, happily, just as they were about to disappear. [43]
>
> They had lost wisdom. [63]
>
> Once again, wisdom had been lost. [64]
>
> It's bad that wisdom should be getting lost. [190]

But if in this context "wisdom" refers to a clearly unassailable and unalterable understanding of man's relation to nature, in the literature produced by the Holocaust the need to understand is rooted in man's relation to man.

For the tribe, home is the place where one chooses to stop walking and remain for a period of time. For the survivor, home is where one was born. But to return home is to encounter a maze of imponderable questions studded with (self-)accusations. In Appelfeld's *The Age of Wonders,* the protagonist "felt a desire to knock on one of the doors and say, 'I'm here. Don't you remember me'?" But the one response he gets is not one he wants to hear: "It's not right for you to come here and stir up evil spirits" (1990:233, 267). Such "spirits," as principal *dramatis personae* in grotesque realism (although not excluded from magical realism), contribute to making the return an especially daunting task for the survivor, for whom "home," a now-poignant oxymoron, as a result of a previously unthinkable transformation, is no longer home. Although the return is a universal theme in world literature, dating at least as far back as *The Odyssey,* in Holocaust literature the drama of return takes on a philosophical dimension, eliciting the question of whether one can return to a place once called "home" that has been deliberately purged of one's culture and soul and, therefore, effectively of oneself—one strangely still-living self. For the problem of return is compounded, as we see in what follows, by the question of remaining. "Even the Jewish shops have preserved their outward appearance, like the Lauffer's drapery shop. None of them have survived but their shop is still standing at exactly the same angle as before, perfectly preserved, even the geraniums in their pots. Now a different man is sitting there with a different woman. Strange—they don't look like murderers" (Appelfeld 1990:216-17).

Precisely the problem of complicity, implied in that last unyielding phrase, is the problem that Weisel takes up in *The Town Beyond the Wall.* All of the events of the past explored in this novel are framed by a single fact that defines the present: the protagonist, having returned to a Hungarian town behind the Iron Curtain, is being tortured and interrogated, as though *he* were a criminal. The ironic implication is that a society that cannot, or will not, distinguish between victim and victimizer is itself doomed to (self-)annihilation. The main character returns to the place of his birth without understanding why he has undertaken the journey.[16] Only after he has returned does he realize that his quest is centered on the need to examine the role of the Other—not the killer but the idler. He acknowledges some understanding as to the motivations of both victim and assassin. But the idle spectator has remained a more haunting specter than even that of the murderer.

> Do you understand that I need to understand? To understand the others—the Other—those who watched

us depart for the unknown; those who observed us, without emotion, while we became objects—living sticks of wood—and carefully numbered victims?
This, this was the thing I had wanted to understand ever since the war. Nothing else. How a human being can remain indifferent. [1969:159]

In identifying the spectator as "that Other" (161), Wiesel raises a problem that casts a shadow across Bakhtin's most vital meaning-producing model of human communication: the Self and Other,[17] as individuals engaged in dialogic interaction that presumably affords mutual comprehension, meaning, and greater understanding. Wiesel's identification of the Other (in historically accurate terms) as the spectator, the person who had remained indifferent to human persecution and suffering, raises the issue of an attendant situation that is, however, by definition nondialogic in its basic conception. In this case, there can be no path to greater understanding precisely because there had been no channel opened for possible communication. Yet it is precisely this failing, which is eminently possible and repeatable, that casts a shadow over Bakhtin's essentially optimistic viewpoint: what if, in other words, human beings choose not to speak, and not to speak precisely at the moment when there is the greatest need to do so?

In contrast to Wiesel's relentless probing for answers (which implies in his complex, sometimes strained dialectic the constant pyramiding of new questions), a basic operative principle of Appelfeld's art is an almost unbearable aura of understatement. In *The Age of Wonders,* the events of the Holocaust are subsumed under a single phrase—"Many Years Later When Everything Was Over"—that marks the passage of time between the first and second parts of the book, between "before" and "after." It is thus incumbent upon the reader to approach this novel already cognizant of "everything," in order to be fully receptive to the ominous import of Appelfeld's lyric reflections, as the novelist recalls a past that can never be re-called, ruminating upon times that had been deprived of the carnivalesque sense of renewal and rebirth, which Bakhtin perceives as pervading medieval folk culture, but which decidedly does not inhabit the sphere of Appelfeld's folk.

> I sensed: my own little life, held to its narrow compounds, had escaped from its constraints and approached the threshold of a darkness I did not understand. [1990:36]
>
> Now I knew: the quiet, still days that had filled the rooms of the house with the serenity of small activities, those days were over. [55]
>
> I knew: everything I had once known, my childhood too, was over. [100]
>
> Everything around us was in a state of gay, drugged despair and the bitter smell of the approaching end was already in the air. [134]
>
> Now she understood what she had not understood before: everything was gone, gone forever. She would remain alone, alone forever. [1983:140]
>
> Every now and then her [dead] mother would call . . . and [she] would reply, "Here I am." Of her entire childhood, only this was left. [158]

In such passages, scoured of all passion and emotion, the author depicts a past that, devoid of seed, has been decreed barren and is thus finished and done with; in this new "age of wonders," in which millions of souls had been dispatched as smoke leaving no trace and no possibility for renewal, one can say (in stark contrast to the potential for rebirth that Bakhtin acclaims in medieval folk culture): *"It's all over"* (Appelfeld 1990:269). With stunning simplicity, that trite little phrase stands in sad, bold opposition to the great promise of regeneration, rebirth, and new life promised by the folk culture of earlier times. What remains is now stagnant, passive, and static, promising nothing but a vague, deadening repetition. "Now everything stands there without them, comfortable and homely, bathed in the same familiar light returning every year in its placid provincial rhythm" (217)—a rhythm that, in its very calm, is devoid not only of carnival but of the very potential for carnival, with its joyous promise of rejuvenation and renewal, of more life and new life.

5 / ARCHETYPAL ASPECTS

*For myself, I feel obliged to establish
the actuality of archetypes.*
—Gaston Bachelard [1964:188]

In concluding, I return to a problem raised at the start. For in our considerations of the carnivalesque, an underlying question remains: are we treating a continuum that is in some sense representative of what might be viewed as an anthropological constant? That is, an "anthropologically motivated postulate" (Mukarovsky 1978:56), rooted in a certain reiterative human tendency or impulse that makes its appearance in various guises in virtually all cultures? One might make such an argument, as I have shown previously, on the basis that "there are certain constitutive characteristics of the human species that dispose us to regard the world in a certain way and to make and evaluate art accordingly. . . . There are universals that not only consistently appeal to us as human beings but that also contribute to our being human" (Danow 1987:146). The concept of an anthropological constant may thus be understood as fluid, traversing a spectrum that has been charted in the present context according to a sometimes chimerical polarity, posited in magical realism at one extreme and in grotesque realism at the other. To reiterate my earlier point, however, this is a continuum in which the two poles are in flux, may even curl about each other (like our tail-eating serpent), so that at times they meet and overlap. In *The Lost Steps,* for instance, there is the episode (remarked earlier), in which a leper who has raped a child is shot in the face, resulting in his deformed visage turning into "a bloody mass that was disintegrating, slipping down his chest like melting wax" (Carpentier 1979:201). Magical realism is thus for a brief moment transformed into grotesque realism.[1]

My concern in this study has been to propose the idea (which is not empirically demonstrable) that human beings, in their art making, are animated by a periodic predisposition toward a bright perspective of wide-open potential, balanced by a like but potentially far darker inclination whose immanent linkage I have designated the carnivalesque-grotesque. In this understanding, both impulses represent related features of the same "face," revealing a visage that at times smiles at the potential prospects of the collective human endeavor, but at other moments appears perplexed and horrified at the result of that endeavor, reacting, in effect, to history gone wrong.[2]

The very nature of this study, with its emphases on fundamental oppositions and basic dualities, makes it tempting to construe the basic argument here in accord with Nietzsche's well known doctrine of the Apollonian-Dionysian antinomy, to which, the German philosopher maintains, "art owes its continuous evolution" (1956:19). But the problems that would accrue to succumbing to such an alignment are several. First, Nietzsche argues for a certain "mysterious marriage" (36) between these two interacting artistic impulses. This might appear suitable to a discussion of magical realism, in which there *is* a certain dreamlike quality (attributed by Nietzsche

Archetypal Aspects

to the Apollonian vision) manifested in an often disarmingly serene contemplation of the world—even when declaring the most astounding manifestations of life forces within that world. Likewise, magical realism's healthy inclination toward zestful exaggeration and unlicensed behavior might comfortably be accounted for by the Dionysian view of art and life.

But that same Nietzschean opposition (which is also perceived, significantly, as a union) would find only a strained place, if any, in my discussion of grotesque realism. It would be difficult, indeed crass, to identify the dreamy Apollonian strain of thought with a literature designed to reflect the war experience generally and the Holocaust specifically, and even more inappropriate to associate a literature reflecting those events with the Dionysian vision, which emphasizes the unfettered joys of existence. At best, we would have to skew greatly Nietzsche's joint designations to fit our argument—and the point (whatever it might be) in so doing would surely be lost in the skewing.

Further, while there are certain similarities, as I have argued, existing between magical realism and grotesque realism, when viewed through the powerful refractive prism of the carnivalesque—a prism that reflects partly the Dionysian attitude but only marginally the Apollonian—those similarities do not afford the unified perspective that Nietzsche observes in the "constant conflicts and periodic acts of reconciliation" (19) that adhere to his well known opposition. Although magical realism is indeed a contrapuntal art, embracing both light and dark, grotesque realism, in distinct contrast on this important count, is essentially a single-visioned form expressing the "tragic myth," defined (appropriately enough to our context) by Nietzsche as the "image of all that is awful, evil, perplexing, destructive, ominous in human existence" (8). Clearly, in grotesque realism there can be no room for either joy or reconciliation, since that "myth" came into being with a horror and a force that Nietzsche himself could never have conceived.

Yet, when Nietzsche observes that the "Apollonian consciousness was but a thin veil hiding ... the whole Dionysiac realm" (28), one feels that, *mutatis mutandis,* a similar case could be made for the relations explored in this study between magical realism and its grotesque counterpart. Even Nietzsche's expressive faith in his antinomy's achieving a certain union holds some truth for the present context: "And lo and behold! Apollo found it impossible to live without Dionysos. The elements of titanism and barbarism turned out to be quite as fundamental as the Apollonian element" (34). In other words, as we have seen in magical realism, below the surface of the sleepy generic Caribbean town there lurks the ever-present potential for conflict, hostility, and violence. In effect, the horrific is forever lying in wait, ready to subvert the relatively innocuous power of "magic," a concern that needs to be addressed.

In a critique of Nietzsche's dichotomy, Jung obliquely addresses that concern in his inquiry into "The Apollinian and the Dionysian." There he observes that Nietzsche's thought spans an opposition, exhibiting intensely dark tones "that certainly enhance the effect of the light but allow still blacker depths to be divined" (1971:137). That assessment, in effect, might be seen to reflect the aim of the present investigation as well. Jung goes on to say that Nietzsche "had a pronounced tendency to credit art with a mediating and redeeming role. The problem then remains stuck in aesthetics—the ugly is also 'beautiful,' even beastliness and evil shine forth enticingly in the false glamour of aesthetic beauty" (140-41). For Jung, being "stuck in aesthetics," mired in that "false glamour," means that the possibility of a religious perspective remains entirely ignored. "The aesthetic attitude guards against any real participation, prevents one from being personally implicated, which is what a religious understanding of the problem would mean" (142). Counterposed to Jung's assessment of Nietzsche's argument is Bakhtin's stated position, declared in his first published writing, a two-page, spirited manifesto, "Art and Answerability" (1919): "I have to answer with my own life for what I have experienced and understood in art. . . . Art and life are not one, but they must become united in myself—in the unity of my answerability" (1990:1-2). That position perhaps comes closest to providing a response (which Jung terms "religious" and which others might regard as "spiritual") to the Swiss psychologist's call for the need to take a personal stand with regard to art.

To identify the dualistic carnivalesque model presented here with Nietzsche's twin model would result in a false schematization. Although this study does parallel Nietzsche's investigation of two interacting artistic impulses, and likewise seeks "at least an intuitive comprehension of the mystery which made this conjunction possible" (1956:36), Nietzsche's "conjunction" does not comply with our initial concerns or subsequent findings. Still, in the German philosopher's dichotomy, heralding a fruitful union of opposites from which art is born, there emerges a related clear recognition of the need for a dualistic approach in human thinking (Nietzsche speaks of the need to avoid deriving the arts from a "single vital principle" 97) that is reflected in my view of the carnivalesque as being inherently motivated by both a bright and a dark side. Further, while the dualistic view that he espouses is surely as powerful as the related model of this study, his opposition appears to emphasize less the precarious balance between its two principal exponents, and withholds the kind of evaluative assessment that Bakhtin, in contrast, affords his celebration of the people as manifested in carnival.

For Bakhtin, as noted, the carnivalesque-grotesque finds its *raison d'être* in its ability "to consecrate inventive freedom . . . to liberate from the prevailing point of view of the world. . . [and] offers the chance to have a new outlook on the world, to realize the relative nature of all that exists, and to enter a completely new order of things" (1968:34). Conjured under the notion of a carnivalesque spirit that unites within itself official culture and its unofficial counterpart, the lawful and what is unlawful, the rational and the irrational, the carnivalesque model allows, then, for the latter member of each such pair to supersede the primary member, so that the unofficial culture, sponsoring irrationality, license, and lawlessness will temporarily (but presumably not ultimately) triumph. But what is achieved by all this? For Bakhtin, the end result of this toppling of established values for a brief period of time is clearly positive; while the means to achieving that result may remain essentially ambiguous, those means (which is to say, the carnival attitude in its multitudinous manifestations) nevertheless represent an acknowledged reality that provides an inspiration for art. That, after all, has been the point here.

But does that accurate assessment of the pervasive, prominent role of carnival in the making of art account for all that is positive in the carnival attitude or in carnivalized reality? A closer look at Bakhtin's evocation of carnival reveals it to be a popular source of *knowledge*.[3] When Bakhtin speaks of liberating "from the prevailing point of view," of offering "the chance to have a new outlook," of realizing "the relative nature of all that exists," and of entering "a completely new order of things," he is articulating a theory that is essentially epistemological at base, one that seeks new ways of knowing and new approaches to understanding the world and man's place within it. In succinct, humorous formulation, the rationale for the kind of thinking that accommodates the carnivalesque (and, conversely, its realization in life as carnival) is encapsulated by Fuentes: "Put all your ideas on one side of the balance, then put everything that negates them on the other, and then you'll be closer to the truth" (1992:230). In effect, that pithy remark incorporates the notion of carnival, writ small, with its essential oppositions between official and unofficial culture, between what is lawful and unlawful. It also emphasizes the underlying rationale for juxtaposing seemingly irreconcilable pairs: in a word, to *learn* whatever we can from the unlikely juxtapositions that afford us a periodically carnivalized reality, which in turn is manifested in art as the carnivalesque.

In his well known early assessment of Bakhtin's thought, V.V. Ivanov points out: "Bakhtin insisted on the length of the path separating carnival from 'primitive' rituals. This does not prevent him from recognizing that the carnival tradition, in Shakespeare, for example . . . has its roots in the prehistoric past . . . that is, goes back to cultural archetypes" (1974: 339-40). In the course of this study the implicit aim has been to suggest that the carnival tradition may be traced (well beyond Shakespeare) through seemingly disparate works of twentieth-century narrative that on the surface may appear to have little in common but that are, nevertheless, derived in varying degrees from precisely that tradition that occupied Bakhtin in his study of medieval and Renaissance folk culture.

Concerning Shakespeare, Bakhtin writes: "The semantic treasures Shakespeare embedded in his works were created and collected through the centuries and even millennia: they lay hidden in the language, and not only in the literary language, but also in those strata of the popular language that before Shakespeare's time had not entered literature, in the diverse genres and forms of speech communication, in the forms of a mighty national culture (primarily carnival forms) that were shaped through millennia, in theater-spectacle genres ... in plots whose roots go back to prehistoric antiquity, and, finally, in forms of thinking" (1986:5). In this study, I have concentrated upon the carnival forms that "were shaped through millennia" and that, as I have tried to show, still play an extraordinarily significant role in modern literary creation. My concluding concerns focus upon a necessarily delimited consideration of certain "forms of thinking" that are essentially at the core of art making.

One such concern that I have taken up in my discussion of magical realism is the universal preoccupation with time. No narrative can do without it; no people have managed to dispense with at least some consideration of it or reaction to it. Human conceptions of time frequently draw upon our capacity for figurative thinking. Thus different peoples may conceive of time as linear, circular, or cyclical. Each of these conceptions derives from metaphors that are geometric in nature. Yet, as Edmund Leach points out: "There is nothing intrinsically geometrical about time as we actually experience it." Moreover, in some primitive cultures, "time is experienced as something discontinuous, a repetition of repeated reversal, a sequence of oscillations between polar opposites: night and day, winter and summer, drought and flood, age and youth, life and death. In such a scheme the past has no 'depth' to it, all past is equally past; it is simply the opposite of now" (1961:126). In other words, instead of saying that time extends linearly from an infinite past to an infinite future, or that it moves in circular or cyclical fashion, time may also be conceived as moving back and forth, like a pendulum, in a series of alternations between dissimilar events that includes most strikingly the distinguishing moments between life and death.

In the magical realist texts discussed here, we have encountered such conceptions of time (including the linear model, implicitly present in the "modern" approach to chronology that conceives of events as taking place in sequential order). In Carpentier's *The Lost Steps,* the protagonist, who travels back in time and deep into the jungle, encounters a young Indian woman who regards time as existing only in the present. For her, all of the past is "equally past"; there is only now—a present that is neither intellectualized, romanticized, nor idealized but that is simply lived in the most basic biological way, "without the chains of yesterday, without thinking of tomorrow" (1979:160). For the enamored protagonist, however, time is hopelessly and irreversibly linear; he is far too "civilized" to change.

The sense of time as circular is felt in magical realist texts by the primitive tribesman as well as the sophisticated individual. In Allende's *Of Love and Shadows,* the circular movement of time is encompassed by the story of a single family, in which one generation makes its escape from Europe and Franco's Spain, while the next seeks refuge fifty years later from the torturous regime of Pinochet's Chile in a now more settled Europe. "He imagined himself unlocking the door with the same turn of the wrist his mother had used to lock it almost half a century before, and he felt as if during that time his family had wandered in a great circle" (1988:278). Likewise, wandering in a circle in Vargas Llosa's *The Storyteller* is the family of primitive tribe members, for whom "history marches neither forward nor backward; it goes around and around in circles, repeats itself" (1990:240). In both cases, that of the Spanish-Chilean family returning to Europe and that of the Indians picking up and walking once again, the result is the same: diaspora. Being scattered, rootless, homeless, remains typical of "the enormous wave of nomads that characterized [the] age: expatriates, emigres, exiles, refugees" (Allende 1988:276). This parade, too, is part of the twentieth-century carnival—that part that is for the most part dark and grim.[4] At its grimmest, affording the darkest possible perspective, a new set of metaphors emerges, far different from those derived from geometry: "Time is no longer abstraction, but a river of blood and death, running into a sea of death and blood" (Wiesel 1967:41).

Offering a veritable compendium of possibility for chronicling the passage of time, *One Hundred Years of Solitude,* a classic instance of magical realism, conceives of time in multitudinous ways: as capable of (carnivalesque) reversal ("It's as if time had turned around and we were back at the beginning" Gárcia Márquez 1971:185); as repetitive ("It's as if the world were repeating itself" 276); as circular ("Time was not passing . . . but . . . was turning in a circle" 310); as fragmented ("time also stumbled and had accidents and could therefore splinter and leave an eternalized fragment in a room" 322); as translucent (affirming "the scientific possibility of seeing the future showing through in time as one sees what is written on the back of a sheet of paper through the light" 360); as coexistent (having "concentrated a century of daily episodes in such a way that they coexisted in one instant" 382). That last possibility is reiterated by Allende: "We believe in the fiction of past, present, and future, but it may also be true that everything happens simultaneously" (1986:432). The whole range of possibility in magical realism is summed up by her thus: "The past and the future formed part of a single unit, and the reality of the present was a kaleidoscope of jumbled mirrors where everything and anything could happen" (82). But, in contrast to this great virtuosity displayed by Time in magical realism, in grotesque realism it moves inexorably, scythe in hand, in pure linear fashion emanating from the cruel presumption that innocent life need be put to inevitable, premature death.

As a final, contrastive point of view, let us consider again Leach's contrary stand: "If there is nothing in the principle of the thing, or in the nature of our experience, to suggest that time must necessarily flow past at constant speed, we are not required to think of time as a constant flow at all. Why shouldn't time slow down and stop occasionally, or even go into reverse?" (1961:133). With this seemingly paradoxical point (distressing perhaps only to our too-civilized selves), Bakhtin, oddly, might agree, for he makes a like paradoxical point of his own: "It turns out that every truly significant step forward is accompanied by a return to the *beginning* ('primitiveness'), or more exactly to a *renewal of the beginning.* Only *memory,* not forgetfulness, can go forward. Memory returns to the beginning and renews it" (1974:293). Yet the seeming paradox of such views can be resolved on several levels. First, from the perspective of our present topic, with its emphasis on recurrence and renewal, this idea conforms with the principle of the carnivalesque, which also adheres to a concern with origins and a corresponding primordial sense of return to those origins. Second, from the viewpoint of the Russian semiotician Yury Lotman, who defines culture as collective memory, Bakhtin's argument serves to support, albeit obliquely, the notion of culture as an ongoing and developing project that likewise depends on the preservation of the past for fruitful humanistic development in the future. Third, such view finds its repeated literary (that is, poetic) reflection; for instance, in Ernesto Sabato's *The Tunnel* (1950), where the reader is told that "life is a process of constructing future memories" (1988:90), and in *The Lost Steps,* where there is a tavern with the "delightfully absurd name: *Memories of the Future*" (Carpentier 1979:116). Last, Bakhtin here appears to echo and corroborate arguments that belong to Jung.

In establishing at least a tentative correlation between the thought of Bakhtin and that of Jung, we need draw upon another related idea of Bakhtin's, which he himself developed only barely: namely, his conception of what he refers to as "Great Time." Within his writings we find only fugitive reference to this notion, as in the following isolated context concerning Gogol, where it is argued that "Gogol's images and plot situations are *immortal*; they exist in Great Time. A phenomenon that belongs to profane time may be purely negative, only hateful; but in Great Time it is *ambivalent* and always *beloved, as involved in existence*" (1974:296; italics added). From the perspective of this study, it may be argued that the concept of carnival itself might well occupy a place within Bakhtin's notion of Great Time, as a universal ("immortal") phenomenon "beloved" by the people because of its "ambivalence" as well as its corresponding "involvement in existence." Its ambivalent quality has been a focal point here all along, while the latter aspect is confirmed by carnival's typifying drive and motivation, intimately tied to the need in life for revivification and revitalization.

The concluding phrase of the incomplete, elliptical essay, which is probably the last thing Bakhtin ever wrote, reads thus: "The problem of *great time*" (1986:170). That problem is ceded to others to resolve—in the sense of affording the concept a broad but succinct formulation and attendant understanding. Here I will note only that the expression suggests the kind of concern that was a lifelong preoccupation of

Archetypal Aspects 149

Bakhtin: the spiritual idea that all utterances are linked, extending from the distant primordial past into the farthest reaches of the future. Thus, in regard to literature, Bakhtin writes: "A work of literature . . . is revealed primarily in the differentiated unity of the culture of the epoch in which it was created, but it cannot be closed off in this epoch: its fullness is revealed only in *great time*" (5). The same can be said, perhaps even more appropriately, of those archetypal ideas, including carnival, that have achieved a certain longevity, that, according to Jung's thinking, have outlasted all other "texts" in their resilience and productivity as the great resource of the human psyche—both in its efforts at survival and in that other great, related project of making art.

What I tentatively posited in this chapter's opening paragraph as an "anthropological constant" is related to Jung's concept of the collective unconscious, which postulates that there are certain experiences belonging to the human psyche that are transpersonal, exceeding the limits of individual experience and extending to that of the race as a whole. Jung refers to the collective unconscious variously as "those immemorial patterns of the human mind, which we have not acquired but have inherited from the dim ages of the past," as having the quality of a "supra-individual psyche," and as bearing "the ancestral heritage of possibilities of representation, [which] is not individual but common to all men" (1960:149-50, 152). Further, he posits: "The contents of the collective unconscious . . . are known as *archetypes*," which he regards as "primordial types, that is . . . universal images that have existed since the remotest times" (1959:4-5). In drawing upon such understandings, we may conclude that the "contents" of the collective unconscious are, then, anthropologically constant in the related meanings Jung gives to these expressions.

In speaking of the "protagonist of carnival," by which he means the people of the marketplace, Bakhtin remarks: "The heart of the matter is not in the subjective awareness but in the *collective consciousness* of their eternity, of their earthly, historic immortality as a people, and of their continual renewal and growth" (1968:250; italics added). Jung speaks of a collective unconscious, Bakhtin of a "collective consciousness." The difference between these two designations is essentially negligible for our concerns, since as Jung explains, archetypes, whose "essential being is unconscious to us," are nonetheless "the dominants that emerge into consciousness as universal ideas" (1960:215, 218). In the present context, it appears reasonable to suppose that carnival is one such universal idea that has emerged into consciousness, whether along the route charted by Jung or by some other. In terms of culturally significant artifacts, the archetype is also referred to by Jung (at an early stage of his thinking) as a "primordial image" (136), as the raw material, we might say, from which art is made. My purpose, in the course of this literary investigation, has been precisely to explore the emergence of certain "dominants" as linked motivating forces in works of twentieth-century literature that might otherwise appear perhaps only obscurely related, if at all.

In literary terms, the dominant may be understood as "the focusing component of a work of art [which] rules, determines, and transforms the remaining components. It is the dominant which guarantees the integrity of the structure" (Jakobson 1971:82). Conversely, "a work enters into literature and takes on its own literary function through this dominant" (Tynjanov 1971:72). In Jungian terms, dominant features of the collective unconscious that "emerge into consciousness as universal ideas," or archetypes, are also designated as "ideas that have always existed, that can be found

Archetypal Aspects 151

again in the most diverse minds and in all epochs, and are therefore not to be mistaken for inherited ideas" (1960:151). The archetype is thus understood as an essentially collective, universal, and regularly occurring phenomenon (134). Jung also equates it to "primordial forms . . . of psychic reaction" (135). Here we may reasonably ask, Reaction to what? One justified response might affirm that, among other possibilities, Jung's notion of primordial forms of psychic reaction may well refer to unofficially touted modes of temporary carnivalized behavior that *react* in primordial fashion to officially sanctioned modes of social conduct. Thus Jung writes: "Just as his instincts compel man to a specifically human mode of existence, so the archetypes force his ways of perception and apprehension into specifically human patterns" (133). The argument of this book has been that the carnival attitude, represented as the carnivalesque in literary production, is precisely one such human pattern. Likewise, when Jung refers to "archetypal modes of perception" (135), those modes may, in fact, serve to distinguish between manifestations of official and unofficial culture, the latter finding a time-honored social response, as Bakhtin argues, in the people's collective reaction within the ancient folk tradition commonly referred to as carnival.

This is not to say that carnival, or the carnivalesque, is to be construed as an archetype. The present chapter is titled as it is purposely. As Jung points out: "The archetypal representations (images and ideas) mediated to us by the unconscious should not be confused with the archetype as such." Rather, it is more accurate to say that the carnivalesque should be perceived as an "archetypal representation," since "it seems probable . . . that the real nature of the archetype is not capable of being made conscious, that it is transcendent" (213).[5] While its "real nature" may be transcendent, the effects of the archetype are clearly realized and perceived in human art making and ritual that include the practice of carnival as ritual and its manifestation in literature as art.

Further, Jung writes: "The concept of the archetype, which is an indispensable correlate of the idea of the collective unconscious, indicates the existence of definite forms in the psyche which seem to be present always and everywhere." The carnivalesque, with *its* "indispensable correlate," the grotesque, is one such "definite form" of what Jung also refers to as "categories of the imagination" or "primordial thoughts" (1959:42-43). My goal has been to reveal such categories or thoughts as fully developed, universal literary themes, filtered through the dualistic concept of the carnivalesque-grotesque.

In defining the archetype, Jung argues that certain human experiences have attained a kind of transcendence: "Endless repetition has engraved these experiences into our psychic constitution, not in the form of images filled with content, but at first only as *forms without content,* representing merely the possibility of a certain type of perception and action" (48).[6] What is problematic, as well as of interest, is that Jung posits a sign bearing a signifier but without a corresponding signified. For him, evidently, the ancient concept of a sign being constituted of a signifier and signified is subordinated to his concept of the archetype as existing eternally *in potentia,* whose form is (paradoxically, from a semiotic point of view) both empty and primordial—awaiting the meaning that individuals living collectively in history will eventually provide it—a meaning that is constantly in flux but whose essence is always the same.

"The archetype is spirit or pseudo-spirit: what it ultimately proves to be depends on the attitude of the human mind" (Jung 1960:206). In other words, while the archetype's "essential being is unconscious to us" (215), it is always there

Archetypal Aspects 153

as the purest and rawest material from which art is made, as "a formative principle of instinctual power" (212). In this sense, we may understand the archetype as being a form devoid of content, a sign whose signifier does not readily afford a corresponding signified, until such time as the artist imbues it with meaning. One way by which meaning is imbued is through the artistic exploration of the carnival attitude in all its possible, varied manifestations.

Finally, Jung argues: "We must, however, constantly bear in mind that what we mean by 'archetype' is in itself irrepresentable, but has effects which make visualizations of it possible, namely, the archetypal images and ideas." An example of that kind of effect, making possible its "visualization" or, better, its artistic representation, is the carnival attitude that Bakhtin first explored in relation to medieval folk culture. As Jung goes on to say: "We meet with a similar situation in physics: there the smallest particles are themselves irrepresentable, but have effects from the nature of which we can build up a model. The archetypal image, the motif or mythologem, is a construction of this kind" (214). And so, we might add, is the carnivalesque-grotesque, whose effects have allowed us to construct the dualistic model that has been built up here.

NOTES

1 / LITERARY MANIFESTATIONS

1. The practice in this book is to place the original date of publication of a work in parentheses immediately following its first mention only. The date following all subsequent citations refers to the text cited in the present work and is noted, with full bibliographical information, in Works Cited.

2. Carnival is rendered in particularly stunning literary imagery in the following passage, in which carnival is depicted as "a general transfiguration" that does not simply begin on a certain day but "explodes" onto everyday life—

> in orange yellow and mandarin yellow; in canary yellow and frog green; in garnet red, robin red, and Chinese-box red; in doublets checkered in indigo or saffron, badges and cockades, peppermint-stick and barber-pole stripes, bicorne hats and plumes, iridescence of silks swirling within eddies of satins and ribbons, Turkish dress and fantastic costumes—with such a blast of cymbals and clappers, of drums, tambourines, and bugles, that all the pigeons of the city rose as a single flight darkening the sky for seconds as they took wing to distant parts. All at once, adding their symphony to that of the flags and pennants, lanterns and lamps came alight on warships, frigates, cargo boats, fishing smacks—their crews in costume . . . [who] set off sparklers, skyrockets, and a fireworks display that culminated in bursts of girandoles and Roman candles. . . .

Everybody was talking, hawking, bawling, brawling, flattering, flirting, singing, soliciting. . . . [Carpentier 1988:67-69]

By contrast, the following passage might be better understood as a figurative description of the carnival *attitude*: "All the bourgeois norms had come tumbling down. . . . A great pastoral ball . . . was being planned. . . . An air of license, of fantasy, of disorder swept the city" (Carpentier 1989:83-84).

3. Gárcia Márquez further explains "this outsized reality" in his 1982 Nobel Lecture, as being "a reality not of paper, but one that lives within us and determines each instant of our countless daily deaths, and that nourishes a source of insatiable creativity, full of sorrow and beauty. . . . Poets and beggars, musicians and prophets, warriors and scoundrels, all creatures of that unbridled reality, we have had to ask but little of imagination, for our crucial problem has been a lack of conventional means to render our lives believable" (1983:17).

4. The point is illustrated in the following account of the war years: "She would tell him about her adventures on the plains: a drunken peasant woman had tried to hit her, a peasant had set his dog on her, a passerby had tried to rob her of the clothes she had taken to barter. She spoke simply, as if she were recounting everyday experiences" (Appelfeld 1983:85).

5. Vargas Llosa provides the following colorful, telling image: "He had two shotguns and so many bandoleers around his neck that they looked like festive carnival necklaces" (1985:269). What is "festive" here, of course, is the carnival of shooting and death.

6. In drawing upon his own Janus face image, "at once Dionysiac and Apollonian" (an opposition to which I will return), Nietzsche comes to the curious conclusion that "whatever exists is both just and unjust, and equally justified in both." Even more curious, he caps his "formula" (as he calls it) with a Gogolian expostulation ("What a world!") that only enhances the confusion (1956:65).

7. In the literature of what might well seem like another age (from what had been just two decades prior), the town square will

serve as the place from which are herded an entire population to the concentration camp and extermination. "The loudspeaker began braying lengthy instructions about going to the right and going to the left, forming in groups of fifty, forming in groups of one hundred . . . standing and waiting" (Begley 1992:133).

8. In his discussion of Menippean satire, which "accorded great importance to the *nether world,*" Bakhtin notes the emergence of the ancient preoccupation with the "resurrection" of the dead: "Here was born that special genre of 'dialogues of the dead,' widespread in European literature of the Renaissance, and in the seventeenth and eighteenth centuries" (1984:116)—and which appears as well in Rulfo's modern literary text that derives of course from what preceded it.

Also gliding across the bounds between the living and the dead, in a more profound existential and metaphysical sense, is Malcolm Lowry's magnificent novel *Under the Volcano* (1947), which takes place on the Day of the Dead (the one day in the year, in Mexico, "when the dead are permitted to live"), with its ghoulish carnival atmosphere replete with celebratory "chocolate skulls . . . chocolate skeletons, chocolate, yes, funeral wagons" (1962:339).

All such flitting between this world and the next perhaps finds its summative expression in Isabel Allende's impressive first novel, *The House of the Spirits* (1982), in which the grandmother spends a lifetime communicating with the dead, explaining to her little granddaughter at the moment of her own death "that if she could easily communicate with those from the Hereafter, she was absolutely convinced that afterward she would be able to do the same with those of the Here-and-Now" (1986:290). In such manner are the (nonexistent) borders between the living and the dead repeatedly glided over in what amounts to a dualistic model in which communication involving spirits can be effected from this world to the next, and vice versa.

9. In *Pedro Paramo,* after the murder of a parent, there is a similar instance of wholesale vengeance, governed by a like code, and again wreaked by the hero of the tale upon virtually everyone within range. "Pedro Paramo caused such a slaughter after his father was shot. . . . [He] couldn't find out who fired the bullet, so he took his revenge on everybody" (Rulfo 1969:77-78). Bearing resonant overtones in this passage that can be seen to stretch at least as

far back as *The Odyssey,* revenge, as a recurrent literary theme reflecting a recurrent preoccupation, is evidently a universal, transcultural, *human* predilection that finds its place in the unofficial world of the carnivalesque rather than in the official realm of law.

2 / THE CARNIVALESQUE-GROTESQUE

1. And yet, laughter, too, has its limitations: "Who was the first to laugh? Nobody knows. But someone began. 'We are memorial candles,' he screams, and they laugh. '*We* didn't die, *they* did!' And they laugh, still swinging their arms in all directions. Their faces twist with laughter.... Laughter. And time flies. Backward. Toward the past, toward there. Where they all are frozen. The laughter stops" (Kaniuk 1972:236-37).

2. Thus Wiesel writes: "The man who chooses death is following an impulse of liberation from the self; so is the man who chooses madness.... The choice of madness is an act of courage" (1969:100-101).

To the question, And if God were mad? we get the stunning answer: "That would explain so much" (148). Along a similar line of thought, we find that idea expressed in much harsher terms: "There the gods designed Hell, but here, in Hell itself, God himself was designed" (Kaniuk 1972:310). Another related notion is put forward by Gárcia Márquez in the words of a deranged priest, who proclaims that "the devil had probably won his rebellion against God, and that he was the one who sat on the heavenly throne" (1971:178).

3. Let me briefly make the case. Bakhtin argues that "the grotesque rejects obviousness and the world 'of what is self-evident' for the sake of the surprises and unanticipated quality of truth. It appears to say that good is to be expected not from the stable and the customary but from a 'miracle.' The grotesque contains the popular renewing and life-affirming idea" (1974:295). In Gárcia Márquez, we encounter the passage: "The afternoon was dying with intense pink clouds and the uproar of parrots and monkeys on

the opposite shore.... Father Angel thought that every afternoon at that instant the town went through the miracle of transfiguration" (1980:50). Bakhtin's notion of a "life-affirming idea" as well as the sense of an occasional "miracle" are immanent to such magical realist texts.

4. Likewise, in seeking a certain "expansion" of this project, certain works discussed under the Latin American rubric may not be considered, strictly speaking, magical realist. But, in both chosen literary forms, what should prove interesting, as Bakhtin and others have argued, are not the borders per se that serve to divide, limit, and delimit, but the ability to traverse those borders; it is not the frames themselves that deserve our contemplation so much as the possible breaking of frames.

5. Perhaps nowhere do we get a greater sense of Stalin's lurking presence than in the following telling passage of the people's blind reliance on the leader's infinite wisdom: "For the only thing that gave us security on earth was the certainty that he was there, invulnerable to plague and hurricane...invulnerable to time, dedicated to the messianic happiness of thinking for us, knowing that we knew that he would not take any decision for us that did not have our measure, for he had not survived everything because of his inconceivable courage or his infinite prudence but because he was the only one among us who knew the real size of our destiny" (Gárcia Márquez 1977:99).

6. The most stunning instance of this immediate and sudden reaction takes place when the general serves up his one friend, lately supposed a traitor, at and *for* dinner to all the other suspected conspirators (119).

7. We find an even more macabre example of the dictators' "dance of death" in Isabel Allende's *Of Love and Shadows*: "Those governments exchanged information, prisoners, and corpses. In such transactions, there were at times too many dead on one side and too many identity cards on the other, causing considerable confusion when it came time to identify the victims. Thus people were arrested in one country, only to turn up dead in another under a different name, and families who wanted to bury their dead had been known to receive a stranger's body" (1988:282).

8. Equally grotesque is Wiesel's description of a small child elevated through sheer whimsy to a position of power and control over a suffering and anguished adult population. "Well fed and warmly dressed, the little prince strolled among the barracks, inspiring envy, fear, pity. He possessed the power of life and death. ... They feared his anger for it was like that of those in command" (1969:61). In effect, we are again afforded (in relative microcosm) an anatomy of dictatorship. "The little prince: he had reigned over a kingdom of old men, had imposed his law, his moods, his will upon them. He had spoken to them as a master, conscious of his superiority, of his absolute powers. One word from him announced hope or the death of hope. His power illustrated the grotesque side of the situation: thousands of men trembled before an urchin playing games" (71).

9. Also insisting that the individual is morally obligated to take a stand, Primo Levi observes that the concentration camp inmates "sensed that what had happened around them and in their presence, and in them, was irrevocable. Never again could it be cleansed; it would prove that man, the human species—we, in short—had the potential to construct an infinite enormity of pain, and that pain is the only force created from nothing, without cost and without effort. It is enough not to see, not to listen, not to act" (1989:86).

10. In *Wartime Lies* (1992), Louis Begley chronicles the destruction of the Warsaw ghetto, as people crowded onto rooftops to watch the spectacle, "the first real entertainment the Germans had provided in all this sad time. . . . Occasional bets were made on how long it would be until the whole place was one black pile of rubble, and whether any Jews would be left alive inside it. . . . All of Warsaw was watching. . . the level of joviality was never again so high" (1992:92-93).

That sense of "joviality," of a gruesome carnivalized reality, also makes its grotesque appearance in *Babi Yar* (1966; subtitled "A Document in the Form of a Novel"), where looting is described as having reached grandiose proportions, amidst grim carnivalesque reversals.

> By morning all the shop-windows had been knocked out and figures could be seen . . . carrying rolls of carpet and piles of

crockery, bundles of children's satchels and even curtains out of the theatres. And there were Germans busy among them as well. They chased the looters away, uttering threats and clouting people over the head, and then started looting themselves. It was like an overturned ant-heap—everybody was carrying something somewhere. . . . They were dragging stuff . . . into their new flats, turning them into store-rooms. There was a tale about a workman who moved from the basement to the first floor and collected twelve grand pianos, stacking them one on top of the other. [Anatoli 1971:55-56]

How easily the tentative bounds are crossed between torturer and spectator is documented in D.M. Thomas' *The White Hotel*, where a jeer at the victims or the theft of their remaining meager belongings is an equally heinous act performed by those watching the procession of innocents condemned to summary execution. "An old woman in a dirty headscarf darted out from a courtyard, snatched up the case and ran with it back into the yard. . . . Two muscular men stepped out from behind the wall and barred the entrance. There was a whole pile of goods behind the men. . . . Faces were pressed to the windows of houses, looking down on the dense mass of migrants. Some looked sorry for them, but others laughed and jeered" (1982:271). (The "documentary" account from which this episode is derived originally appears in Anatoli 1971:70.)

The answer to such barbarism, if one is morally equipped to act in accord with the idea, is expressed in Ilse Aichinger's *Herod's Children* (1948):

> You keep only what you give away. Give them what they take from you, for they grow poorer thereby. Give them your toys, your coats, your lives. Give everything away. He who takes loses. Laugh when they tear the clothes from your bodies and the caps from your heads. Laugh at the surfeited, at the contented who have lost hunger and restlessness—man's most precious gifts. Give away your last piece of bread to guard yourself from hunger; give away your last bit of property and remain restless. Throw the gleam in your face to the dark, to strengthen it. [1963:126]

11. To that "aptly posed" formulation, there is (of course) a counter point of view, expressed here in implicit but nonetheless

direct response by Vargas Llosa: "What did he think, that war was like a carnival, stupid asshole?" (1989:157).

12. Interestingly, in *The World of Silence* (1948), Max Picard terms his concept of Silence, in equally paradoxical terms, "holy uselessness," arguing that "silence points to a state where only being is valid: the state of the Divine" (1952:19-20). Conversely, we might argue that carnival points to a purely human state.

3 / MAGICAL REALISM

1. The closeness and even potential intrusion of the jungle into city life is blithely noted in *The Lost Steps*: "For hundreds of years a struggle had been going on with roots that pushed up the sidewalks and cracked the walls" (Carpentier 1979:42-43). Similarly, in *Eva Luna*, we read: "Agua Santa was a modest village, with adobe, wood, and reed houses lining the roadway; machetes defended it against a wild vegetation that would engulf it in an instant's inattention" (Allende 1989:144).

Yet the threat of the jungle's possible intrusion into modern life has its positive correlative as well. When the kind-hearted, soft-brained maid in Vargas Llosa's *Conversation in the Cathedral* is sought by the police for interrogation in the murder of her mistress (about which she knows nothing), the solution to her predicament is readily provided by her environment: she must disappear. "Nobody would find her in the jungle" (1988:431).

2. "El Dorado, the city of gold of the Indian world" is depicted as a brilliant world of light in Fuentes' *The Campaign*: "Peering over the edge, the old man and the young man saw an entire city slowly coming into view. A city made entirely of light" (1992:86-87).

3. As the anthropologist Edmund Leach argues: "We talk of measuring time, as if time were a concrete thing waiting to be measured; but in fact we *create time* by creating intervals in social life. Until we have done this there is no time to be measured" (1961:135).

4. The possibility of time proceeding in reverse is suggested in a brief exchange in Carpentier's *Concierto Barroco* (1974):

"Good-bye!"

"Until when?"

"Until tomorrow?"

"Or until yesterday." [1988:127]

But temporal reversals are not peculiar to magical realism alone. In the literature of the war, we read that it "seemed that some other time, from some other place, had invaded the town and was silently establishing itself" (Appelfeld 1980:38). That perplexing situation is explained by Wiesel thus: "The clock was turned back for a thousand years: a police dog was the animal that now determined the destiny of the world" ((1967:52-53).

5. Comparable in its silent majesty to those figures encased forever in a block of ice, another such (less likely) "still life" is drawn in *The Autumn of the Patriarch*: "We cut through the gloomy streams of the cloister of the convent of Biscayan nuns, we saw the abandoned cells, we saw the harpsichord adrift in the intimate pool of the music room, in the depths of the sleeping waters of the refectory we saw the whole community of virgins drowned in their dinner places at the long table with the food served on it" (Gárcia Márquez 1977:97).

The depiction of space, too, then, in magical realism necessarily allows for disjointed elements and extraordinary dislocations. Thus, in *One Hundred Years of Solitude,* explorers are astounded to find several miles inland an enormous Spanish galleon. "The whole structure seemed to occupy its own space, one of solitude and oblivion, protected from the vices of time and the habits of the birds. Inside . . . there was nothing but a thick forest of flowers" (Gárcia Márquez 1971:21).

6. For all its apparent gravity, myth is not an entirely serious affair. Carnivalesque aspects also have their place. "Deep in the forest, the lord of demons, Kientibakori, crazy with joy, drank masato and danced. . . . In the forest Kientibakori drank masato, dancing and feasting. His farts were like thunder; his belches like a jaguar's roar" (Vargas Llosa 1990:41,193).

7. Unless this later period in human history be designated "the betrayal" (Kaniuk 1972:215) of the faithful, who "lived inside a narrow ghetto and adored [their] Creator. Who burned them" (86)—this vengeful "God of smokestacks" (231).

8. Thus the indigenous people believe:

Any sort of emotional upheaval had to be controlled, for there is a fatal correspondence between the spirit of man and the spirits of Nature, and any violent disturbance in the former causes some catastrophe in the latter. [Vargas Llosa 1990:16]

By changing their way of life they had upset the order of the world, disoriented the souls of those who had gone. [65]

Anger is a disorder of the world, it seems. If men didn't get angry, life would be better than it is. Anger is what's to blame for their being comets in the sky. With their fiery tails and their wild careering, they threaten to throw the four worlds of the Universe into confusion. [122]

9. A diametrically opposed inclination appears just as deadly, as depicted in the concentration camp escapee's sense of horror and guilt at having deserted his family and his people: "Why did I run away? Why did I have to run away? I abandoned them all and ran away. God will never forgive me" (Appelfeld 1983:66).

10. In a passage in *The Lost Steps,* illustrative of the peculiar mix of Christianity and primitive belief, we find another such "application" of this kind of thought, in which the principle of contiguity is again perceived as a *concrete,* rather than a figurative, association: "the nuns scourged themselves at the feet of a black Christ before the horrifying relic of a bishop's tongue, preserved in alcohol in memory of his eloquence" (Carpentier 1979:61).

11. We find similar evocations in *The Storyteller.* "The strength and the solitude of Nature—the tall trees, the mirror-smooth lagoons, the immutable rivers—brought to mind a newly created world, untouched by man, a paradise of plants and animals. When we reached the tribes, by contrast, there before us was prehistory, the elemental, primeval existence of our distant ancestors: hunters, gatherers, bowmen, nomads, shamans, irrational and animistic.... a world still untamed, the Stone Age, magico-religious

cultures, polygamy, headshrinking ... that is to say, the dawn of human history" (Vargas Llosa 1990:72-73).

12. That generality extends to place as well, as is made explicit in the introductory "Author's Note," in which we are told that the cities and towns of the novel are "mere prototypes" whose features "are common to many countries" (Carpentier 1979:13).

Generality of place is a feature inherent to many magical realist works, whose respective tales are designed to elicit the sense of a common history. Thus, the country in which *Eva Luna* is set also remains unnamed. Instead, the author establishes the setting only vaguely as a country in South America—one inundated with oil (perhaps Venezuela). When historical detail is provided, that information is again essentially "generic," belonging not to any single place but to South America at large, with its myriad governments, dictators, revolutions, and revolutionaries. Perhaps the most spirited assessment of such real and potential havoc is made by an imaginative procuress and brothel keeper in *Eva Luna*: "The best thing about this country, she used to sigh with delight, is that there is enough corruption for everyone" (Allende 1989:124). However, the final word in the matter should likely go to the narrative voice that presents Eva Luna's magical world: "But even allowing for a history of colonization, political bosses, and tyrants, it was the promised land" (211).

13. The feel of that awful repetition in political events, again affording a sense of commonality (if not a certain universality), is likewise conveyed in the following strained speech fragment: "Any moment now we'll get the news that the money for the plot has disappeared. . . . Any moment now the leaders will be accusing each other of being traitors and thieves. Sometimes you get bored with the same things always happening, don't you?" (Vargas Llosa 1988:283).

What those "same things" might be is intimated in Vargas Llosa's characterization of "those South American countries whose history has been nothing but a succession of barrack-room pronunciamentos" and in the cautionary observation: "Let us keep our Republic from turning into what so many other Latin American republics have: a grotesque witches' sabbath where all is chaos, military uprisings, corruption, demagogy" (1985:131, 349).

Gárcia Márquez affords a like sense of tedious repetition in the concluding passage of *In Evil Hour,* where we find encapsulated the making of yet another revolution that is left undepicted at the novel's close but which we can be sure, according to some unwritten law, is certain to occur.

"There was a serenade last night."

"Of lead. . . . There was shooting until just a little while ago."

"Where?"

"All over. . . . It seems they were going crazy looking for clandestine fliers. They said they lifted up the flooring of the barbershop, just by chance[!], and they found guns. The jail is full, but they say men are going into the jungle to join up with guerilla bands." [1980:183]

In this novel, common indiscretions and infidelities within the private sphere are publicized through anonymous lampoons posted at night in a generic sleepy little town, where "nothing ever happens," resulting in corresponding explosions within the public domain. In effect, the novel documents a series of dynamically correlated shifts: from private to public, from peaceful to explosive, from an ordinary "sleepy" life to a carnivalized existence— explained, perhaps, in the following odd assessment: "The only thing that excites [them] is carnival time. They couldn't care less about politics" (Vargas Llosa 1985:381).

14. In a companion hallmark statement, a like unmistakable carnivalesque note is struck, declaring that "the government had fallen, but nothing had changed. So start up the music and dancing, and give me another beer, let's drink to democracy" (Allende 1989:178-79).

15. The kind of reckless determination needed to effect such a "dumb business" is revealed in *One Hundred Years of Solitude,* where one of many revolutionary expeditions is "lost for three months in the jungle in a mad attempt to cross more than a thousand miles of virgin territory in order to proclaim war on the outskirts of the capital" (Gárcia Márquez 1971:141). In this novel, the never-ending wars, revolutions, and counterrevolutions are waged between those designated simply as Conservatives and Liberals, who, we are told, are engaged in fighting "for something that doesn't

have any meaning for anyone" (133), so that "many of them did not even know why they were fighting" (160). Yet, as Vargas Llosa grimly explains: "That is what life is: fleeing an enemy or going out to meet one, knowing that before and behind, in space and in time, there are, and always will be, bullets, wounded, and dead" (1985:386).

16. Those endless lines of mothers seeking word of their sons and loved ones, reminiscent of the darkest days of Stalinism, finds a responsive chord in Anna Akhmatova's cycle of poems "Requiem," a strikingly poignant literary evocation of a similar plight that forms part of a grim chapter in contemporary Russian history.

17. As Vargas Llosa puts it simply: "It's easier to imagine the death of one person than those of a hundred or a thousand....When multiplied, suffering becomes abstract. It is not easy to be moved by abstract things" (1985:384).

18. In *The Lost Steps,* facing the awesome consideration of firing at a leper who has raped and perhaps infected a child with the disease, the protagonist sounds a telling cautionary note: "He ought to be eliminated, done away with, left to the birds of the air. But something in me resisted, as though from the moment my finger tightened on the trigger, *something would be changed forever.* There are acts that throw up walls, markers, limits in a man's existence. And I was afraid of the time that would begin for me the second I turned Executioner" (Carpentier 1979:200-201).

That cautionary note is not heeded, however, in Carpentier's later novel *The Chase,* where a distinctly contrastive point of view is espoused by a professional assassin at the conclusion to a kill: "I am astounded, now, in the face of what lies there, at how simple it is to cut short an existence. Everything seems natural: what once moved has stopped moving...everything that could be felt has been felt, and immobility has only broken a cycle of reiterations" (1990:87). Yet this declaration, sounded by one who sees the violent ending of a life as "natural" and who conceives of life as nothing more than a "cycle of reiterations," appears eminently consonant with a killer's point of view.

19. "And she wanted us to be in the middle of the group. People trying to be on the outside, to get more air and to be able to

get around, were wrong. She didn't care about fresh air; she wanted to live through the night" (Begley 1992:131).

20. That indigenous brand of violence is pivotal in Allende's *Of Love and Shadows*, as the following thematic statement shows: "She had suspected from the beginning that she held the end of a long thread in her hands that when tugged would unravel an unending snarl of horrors" (1988:127). In effect, the subsequent unravelling constitutes the story of the novel, in which we are told that in a Cardinal's office, "The walls were bare except for a cross of barbed wire, a gift from prisoners in a concentration camp," confirming the fact that in this land, too, there was indeed "evidence of unspeakable evil" (220-21).

4 / GROTESQUE REALISM

1. Yet, in another of Appelfeld's works, we find a gross parallelism between the self-imposed diaspora of the tribe and the forced deportation of an entire people, in the following fatally innocent remarks: "The town is getting ready to be transferred. . . . Our sanitorium is emigrating too" (1980:103, 117). Here, in fearful irony, one feels that the innocence of the deportees is no less, while their fate is surely far more terrible, than the innocent meandering of the primitive tribe.

The theme of diaspora, of the seemingly endless wandering of poor lost souls, is a repeated theme of Appelfeld's work (*For Every Sin, To the Land of the Cattails, Tzili: The Story of a Life*), in which the reality of the daily struggle to survive in a hostile environment becomes the only reality, thematically illustrating the notion that "life is nothing but a continuous succession of opportunities for survival" (Gárcia Márquez 1980:105). In curiously meek fashion, certain of Appelfeld's characters, although maimed, actually manage to take advantage of such meager opportunities as might present themselves, and survive.

2. The same kind of mindless verbal repetition or incantation (on the part of a young girl, who also hides out in an attempt to survive the war), as a remedy against fear or pain, and therefore an agent for survival, is documented by Appelfeld: "The air was full

of loud screams, barks, and shots. In her fear she repeated the words she had been taught by the old man, over and over again. The mumbled words calmed her and she fell asleep" (1983:7).

3. The idea of such a "dance" is articulated by Arthur Koestler in a chilling description of torture that clearly draws upon this telling metaphor.

> He staggered back, was caught by the man behind him, flung round to the next one, hit in the stomach, bent double, straightened by a kick against his shin, and sent reeling around and across the circle like a dancer in a grotesque ballet.... While gradually darkness closed in on his mind, torn from time to time by flashes of pain, a strange, almost obscene ecstasy transformed his jumps and jerks in the circle of sweating, snorting, hitting and kicking men into the performance of a ritual dance, with the dull inward thunder of his heart and pulses replacing the beating of the sacred drums. [1968:114]

A "liking for dismal and macabre sensations," expressed in the form of "medieval macabre dances" is noted by Monica Rector as playing a role in early manifestations of Carnival (1984:39).

4. Significantly, the theme of madness is claimed by Bakhtin to be inherent to all forms of the grotesque. Yet he registers an immediate duality: "In folk grotesque, madness is a gay parody of official reason, of the narrow seriousness of official 'truth.' It is a 'festive' madness. In Romantic grotesque, on the other hand, madness acquires a somber, tragic aspect of individual isolation" (1968:39). Concerning the latter contrastive point, the same may be said of grotesque realism, where the sense of isolation is perhaps nowhere greater than when a survivor returns to the town of his birth to confront emptiness and ghosts. ("Ghosts, thronging up from the depths of history. Fearful, silent ghosts." Wiesel 1969:160) For in that isolation and sad confrontation madness lurks, as the practitioners of this literary form well know.

5. Another boy trapped by the war makes similar suppositions:

> Can it really be true that the only thing people have learnt to do to perfection in the whole of their history is to murder each other? ... Century after century, people are killed and rot in the earth, now for one thing and now for another, and

later it turns out that everything was in vain. . . . There was
not the slightest hope, not even a glimmer of hope, of justice
being done. It would never happen. No one would ever do it.
The world was just one big Babi Yar. [Anatoli 1971:151,
165]

Such are a whole generation's common childhood ruminations.

6. A small Asiatic people, the Kalmuks took the opportunity offered by the German occupation to rebel against the Soviets. "Hating the Reds, they joined the Germans who permitted them to loot and rape" (Kosinski 1966:157), and, as the novel suggests, enjoy the war as brutally as they could.

7. This theme is treated cinematically in Liliana Cavani's *The Night Porter* (1973), in which both torturer and victim feel compelled, upon meeting many years after the war, to recreate a mock environment of their shared concentration camp existence.

8. In another Appelfeld novel, the voice of a survivor also becomes the plaint of a suicide: "A man abandons his wife and children, his father and mother. What is he if not a murderer?" (1983:151) In this instance, the speaker cannot live with the fact of his own salvation in the face of so many others' deaths, since "to survive," as one grievous argument has it, "is ultimately to betray the dead" (Neher 1981:219).

9. In this novel, a poetics of the Word intersects nicely with a poetics of the street in the little encounter Bartfuss has with his young daughter.

Now he was afraid of himself, of his silence. He turned to her
and said, "Why did you go out?" He spoke as though to an
irresponsible creature.

"I was bored."

"What did you expect to find in the street?"

"People." [118]

Thus, in the absence of speech that pervades their world, the child still seeks the possibility of human communication.

In contrast, in *Mr. Theodore Mundstock,* a work that offers a profound meditation on an old man's justified fears, terrible

Notes

aloneness, and ironically hopeless preparations for the worst, the street, which he is assigned to sweep, is a place of terror.

> Blue-gray clouds poured down the street and from them came a rattling, thundering, rolling noise. Like a storm raging down the street.
>
> He saw wheels, smelled rubber and gasoline. He saw steel helmets wearing coats with ammunition belts over them. They were on their way to murder. [Fuks 1969:99]

10. Evidently others have a like expectation: "You people were in the camps weren't you? From you we expect something different" (Appelfeld 1983:177). Yet novelistic "fact" may argue for the demands of human nature being everywhere the same.

> The summer sun worked its magic. As if the years in the camps had vanished without a trace. A forgetfulness which was not without humor. Like, for example, the woman who performed night after night, singing, reciting, and exposing her thighs. No one reminded her of her sins in the labor camp. She was now their *carnival queen*. . . . She was in the camp for a full year. . . . And every night she performed for the inmates. [163, 184; italics added]

11. As one illiterate but good-hearted soul puts it in Vargas Llosa's *Conversation in the Cathedral*: "People with brains get to understand each other by talking" (1988:210).

12. The opposite point of view is expressed by Gabriella Coo, an aspiring young actress in Fuentes' *The Campaign,* who is subjected to a gentle irony in her nonetheless laudatory admiration for the Word: "She loved words, said Gabriella Coo; each word had its own life and required the same care as a newborn child. When she opened her mouth . . . and repeated a word—love, pleasure, world, sea—she had to take charge of that word like a mother, like a shepherdess, like a lover . . . convinced that, without her, without her mouth, her tongue, the word would smash against a wall of silence and die forsaken" (1992:155).

Yet the case for silence can also be artfully made: "Like some old, forgotten animal from the beginning of time, silence towers above the puny world of noise. . . . Sometimes all the noise of the world today seems like the mere buzzing of insects on the broad back of silence" (Picard 1952:22-23). Still, as the maker of this metaphor himself forcefully argues, out of silence emerges speech in "the power of silence to create speech" (24).

13. This term was used by the Nazis to describe the policy of secrecy and concealment surrounding the concentration camps (Neher 1981:142).

14. Similarly, in treating Rabelais' use of outlandish numbers, Bakhtin argues (1968:463-65) that they are employed to heighten the sense of the grotesque in a "gay, carnivalesque" way. The more precise the figure, the more absurd that cipher appears; its very exactitude, in other words, elicits doubts of its veracity. By contrast, the numerical detailing found on a scale of horrific magnitude in Holocaust literature affords a sense of the grotesque that is only numbing and electrifying, again indicating a clear opposition between the "gay carnivalesque" and the "degrading grotesque."

Concerning the awful novelty at hand, as Neher points out: "The brutal, planned perfection of 'concentrational' death instituted a new kind of death in the history of humanity. Death at Auschwitz bears comparison with no form of death known from the beginning of history until now. Until the twentieth century, such a death was unthinkable" (1981:143). Wiesel personalizes the point: "Between the death of my father [in Buchenwald] and that of his, no comparison is possible" (1970:20).

15. That severe deprivation amounts, in effect, to an act of "anti-creation," in accord with Carpentier's supposition that we perform a "true act of creation, like Adam, by giving [something new] a name" (1979:205). That same idea is supported as well by Boris Pasternak in *Doctor Zhivago,* and by Fuentes in the telling remark: "By naming her, he created her" (1992:192). Conversely, and this in part defines Bartfuss' dilemma: "Without a name there is no existence" (Kaniuk 1972:214)—a grim notion that is illustrated in the following perverse madhouse drama.

"Wolfovitz, who are you?"

"I am Wolfovitz."

"No. Raise your hand, roll up your sleeve. Look, what's written there?"

"8 ... 1 ... 9 ... 8 ... 7 ... "

"Well, then, who are you?"

"Yes, I am not Wolfovitz. I never was and never will be. I am 81987." [233]

From another singular perspective, things are a lot worse for Bartfuss than his being deprived of affection as a condition of his existence. "I did not fear the ordinary hell of flames and physical suffering but the hell I imagined, and that hell is a place where no one speaks: the place of eternal, total silence forever; never more a voice, never a word" (Fuentes 1992:225). According to this perspective, Bartfuss already exists in Hell.

16. The same can be said of Appelfeld's *The Age of Wonders,* where, in the absence of questioning his motivation, the central character attempts to absorb (over a prolonged period of time) sensuous detail from the past—the town's sights and smells—as best he can.

17. For an expanded discussion of the topic, see Danow 1991:59-74.

5 / ARCHETYPAL ASPECTS

1. A fine cinematic illustration of a like transformation of the carnivalesque into the grotesque is shown in Peter Greenaway's *The Cook, The Thief, His Wife, and Her Lover* (1990), in which there are scenes of pure carnivalesque—Rabelaisian non-stop gorging in a surrealistic restaurant that serves as a metaphor for the world—intermeshed with scenes of cruelty that are grotesque. Thus the woman who reports to the thief that his wife has taken a lover, at first in the restroom of the restaurant and later among the raw cuts of beef, fruits, and vegetables in the kitchen, is herself rewarded with a fork stuck full in her face.

2. Speaking in 1936, Jung, in effect, addressed the problem of "history gone wrong" in his discussion of archetypal behavior manifested in pathological form.

> If thirty years ago anyone had dared to predict that our psychological development was tending towards a revival of the medieval persecutions of the Jews, that Europe would again tremble before the Roman fasces and the tramp of legions, that people would once more give the Roman salute, as two thousand years ago, and that instead of the Christian Cross an archaic swastika would lure onward millions of warriors ready for death—why, that man would have been hooted at as a mystical fool. And today? Surprising as it may seem, all this absurdity is a horrible reality. [1959:48]

3. "Carnival is not time wasted but time filled with profound and rich experience" (Clark and Holquist 1984:302).

4. In accord with the just-cited Latin American view, we find an equally compelling European perspective.

> At that time the great battlefronts were collapsing, and the first refugees were groping their way across the broad fields of snow. Against the vast whiteness they looked like swarms of insects. [Appelfeld 1983:119]

> The snow thawed and the first convoys of refugees poured down the hillsides. [124]

> The cold spring sun exposed them like moles. A motley crew of men, women, and children. [127]

5. Elsewhere, Jung declares emphatically: "One must, for the sake of accuracy, distinguish between 'archetype' and 'archetypal ideas.' The archetype as such is a hypothetical and irrepresentable model" (1959:5 n. 9). Interestingly, and also relevant to the present context, Jung states: "Just as all archetypes have a positive, favourable, bright side that points upwards, so also they have one that points downwards, partly negative and unfavourable" (226). I have been making essentially the same point with regard to such "archetypal ideas" as the spirit of carnival and its representation in literature as the carnivalesque.

6. In presenting numerous angles by which to regard the concept, Jung writes: "Archetypes have, when they appear, a distinctly numinous character which can only be described as 'spiritual,' if 'magical' is too strong a word" (1960:205). Clearly, from the perspective of this study, that expression is not too strong.

WORKS CITED

Aichinger, Ilse. 1963. *Herod's Children*. Cornelia Schaeffer, trans. New York: Atheneum.
Allende, Isabel. 1986. *The House of the Spirits*. Magda Bogin, trans. New York: Bantam.
———. 1988. *Of Love and Shadows*. Margaret Sayers Peden, trans. New York: Bantam.
———. 1989. *Eva Luna*. Margaret Sayers Peden, trans. New York: Bantam.
Anatoli, A. (Kuznetsov). 1971. *Babi Yar*. David Floyd, trans. New York: Pocket Books.
Appelfeld, Aharon. 1980. *Badenheim 1939*. Dalya Bilu, trans. Boston: Godine.
———. 1983. *Tzili: The Story of a Life*. Dalya Bilu, trans. New York: Dutton.
———. 1984. *The Retreat*. Dalya Bilu, trans. New York: Dutton.
———. 1986. *To the Land of the Cattails*. Jeffrey M. Green, trans. New York: Weidenfeld and Nicolson.
———. 1989. *The Immortal Bartfuss*. Jeffrey M. Green, trans. New York: Perennial Library.
———. 1990. *The Age of Wonders*. Dalya Bilu, trans. Boston: Godine.
Asturias, Miguel Angel. 1982. *Mulata*. Gregory Rabassa, trans. New York: Avon.

Babel, Isaac. 1960. *The Collected Stories*. Walter Morison, trans. New York: Meridian.

Bachelard, Gaston. 1964. *The Poetics of Space*. Maria Jolas, trans. New York: Orion Press.

Bakhtin, Mikhail (M.M.). 1968. *Rabelais and His World*. Helene Iswolsky, trans. Cambridge, Mass.: M.I.T. Press.

———. 1974. "The Art of the Word and the Culture of Folk Humor (Rabelais and Gogol')." In *Semiotics and Structuralism: Readings from the Soviet Union*, Henryk Baran, ed., 274-96. White Plains, N. Y.: International Arts and Sciences Press.

———. 1984. *Problems of Dostoevsky's Poetics*. Theory and History of Literature, Vol. 8. Caryl Emerson, trans. and ed. Minneapolis: Univ. of Minnesota Press.

———. 1986. *Speech Genres and Other Late Essays*. Caryl Emerson and Michael Holquist, eds. Vern W. McGee, trans. Austin: Univ. of Texas Press.

———. 1990. *Art and Answerability: Early Philosophical Essays by M.M. Bakhtin*. Univ. of Texas Press Slavic Series, No. 9. Michael Holquist and Vadim Liapunov, eds. Austin: Univ. of Texas Press.

Begley, Louis. 1992. *Wartime Lies*. New York: Ballantine.

Carpentier, Alejo. 1979. *The Lost Steps*. Harriet de Onis, trans. New York: Avon.

———. 1988. *Concierto Barroco*. Asa Zatz, trans. Tulsa: Council Oak Books.

———. 1989. *The Kingdom of This World*. Harriet de Onis, trans. New York: Noonday.

———. 1990. *The Chase*. Alfred Mac Adam, trans. New York: Noonday Press.

Clark, Katerina, and Michael Holquist. 1984. *Mikhail Bakhtin*. Cambridge, Mass.: Harvard Univ. Press.

Danow, David K. 1987. "Jan Mukarovsky's Concept of the Work of Art as Sign." In *Semiotics 1986,* John Deely and Jonathan Evans, eds., 140-48. Lanham, Maryland: Univ. Press of America.

———. 1991. *The Thought of Mikhail Bakhtin: From Word to Culture.* New York: St. Martin's Press.

Desai, Anita. 1990. *Baumgartner's Bombay.* New York: Penguin.

Frazer, Sir James. 1963. *The Golden Bough.* New York: Macmillan.

Fuentes, Carlos. 1992. *The Campaign.* Alfred Mac Adam, trans. New York: Harper Perennial.

Fuks, Ladislav. 1969. *Mr. Theodore Mundstock.* Iris Urwin, trans. New York: Ballantine.

García Márquez, Gabriel. 1971. *One Hundred Years of Solitude.* Gregory Rabassa, trans. New York: Avon.

———. 1977. *The Autumn of the Patriarch.* Gregory Rabassa, trans. New York: Avon.

———. 1980. *In Evil Hour.* Gregory Rabassa, trans. New York: Avon.

———. 1983. "Nobel Lecture." Marina Castaneda, trans. *New York Times,* 6 Feb., p. 4.17.

———. 1984. *Chronicle of a Death Foretold.* Gregory Rabassa, trans. New York: Ballantine.

Ivanov, Viach. Vs. (V.V.). 1974. "The Significance of M.M. Bakhtin's Ideas on Sign, Utterance, and Dialogue for Modern Semiotics." In *Semiotics and Structuralism: Readings from the Soviet Union,* Henryk Baran, ed., 310-67. White Plains, N.Y.: International Arts and Sciences Press.

———. 1984. "The Semiotic Theory of Carnival as the Inversion of Bipolar Opposites." In *Carnival!* by Umberto

Eco, V.V. Ivanov, Monica Rector, 11-35. Berlin: Mouton.
Jakobson, Roman. 1971. "The Dominant." *Readings in Russian Poetics: Formalist and Structuralist Views*, Ladislav Matejka and Krystyna Pomorska, eds., 82-87. Cambridge, Mass.: MIT Press.
Jung, Carl. 1959. *The Archetypes and the Collective Unconscious*. Vol. 9, Part I of *The Collected Works of C.G. Jung*. Bollingen Series XX, Sir Herbert Read, Michael Fordham, and Gerhard Adler, eds. New York: Pantheon Books, 1959.
———. 1960. *The Structure and Dynamics of the Psyche*. Vol. 8 of *The Collected Works of C.G. Jung*. New York: Pantheon Books.
———. 1971. *Psychological Types*. Vol. 6 of *The Collected Works of C.G. Jung*. Princeton, N.J.: Princeton Univ. Press.
Kaniuk, Yoram. 1972. *Adam Resurrected*. Seymour Simckes, trans. London: Chatto and Windus.
Koestler, Arthur. 1968. *Arrival and Departure*. New York: Bantam.
Kosinski, Jerzy. 1966. *The Painted Bird*. New York: Pocket Books.
Lachmann, Renate. 1987. *Bakhtin and Carnival: Culture as Counter-Culture*. Minneapolis: Univ. of Minnesota Center for Humanistic Studies, Occasional Papers, No. 14.
Leach, E.R. 1961. *Rethinking Anthropology*. London School of Economics Monographs on Social Anthropology, No. 22. London: Univ. of London, Athlone Press.
Levi, Primo. 1989. *The Drowned and the Saved*. Raymond Rosenthal, trans. New York: Vintage.
Lowry, Malcolm. 1962. *Under the Volcano*. Harmondsworth: Penguin.

Works Cited

Malinowski, Bronislaw. 1954. *Magic, Science and Religion*. New York: Anchor Books.

Mukarovsky, Jan. 1978. *Structure, Sign, and Function: Selected Essays by Jan Mukarovsky*. John Burbank and Peter Steiner, eds. and trans. New Haven: Yale Univ. Press.

Neher, André. 1981. *The Exile of the Word: From the Silence of the Bible to the Silence of Auschwitz*. David Maisel, trans. Philadelphia: Jewish Publication Society.

Nietzsche, Friedrich. 1956. *The Birth of Tragedy* and *The Genealogy of Morals*. Francis Golffing, trans. New York: Anchor Books.

Patterson, David. 1992. *The Shriek of Silence: A Phenomenology of the Holocaust Novel*. Lexington: Univ. Press of Kentucky.

Picard, Max. 1952. *The World of Silence*. Stanley Godman, trans. Chicago: Henry Regnery.

Rabon, Israel. 1990. *The Street*. Leonard Wolf, trans. New York: Four Walls Eight Windows.

Rector, Monica. 1984. "The Code and Message of Carnival: 'Escolas de Samba.' " In *Carnival!* Umberto Eco, V.V. Ivanov, Monica Rector, 37-165. Berlin: Mouton.

Rulfo, Juan. 1969. *Pedro Paramo*. Lysander Kemp, trans. New York: Grove Press.

Sabato, Ernesto. 1988. *The Tunnel*. Margaret Sayers Peden, trans. New York: Ballantine.

Solzhenitsyn, Alexander. 1968. *Cancer Ward*. Nicholas Bethell and David Burg, trans. New York: Bantam.

Terras, Victor. 1991. *A History of Russian Literature*. New Haven: Yale Univ. Press.

Thomas, D.M. 1982. *The White Hotel*. New York: Pocket Books.

Tynjanov, Jurij. 1971. "On Literary Evolution." In *Readings in Russian Poetics: Formalist and Structuralist Views*, Ladislav Matejka and Krystyna Pomorska, eds., 66-78. Cambridge, Mass.: MIT Press.

Vargas Llosa, Mario. 1985. *The War of the End of the World.* Helen Lane, trans. New York: Avon.

———. 1988. *Conversation in the Cathedral.* Gregory Rabassa, trans. New York: Noonday Press.

———. 1989. *The Real Life of Alejandro Mayta.* Alfred MacAdam, trans. New York: Vintage.

———. 1990. *The Storyteller.* Helen Lane, trans. New York: Penguin.

———. 1991. *In Praise of the Stepmother.* Helen Lane, trans. New York: Penguin Books.

Wiesel, Elie. 1967. *The Gates of the Forest.* Frances Frenaye, trans. New York: Avon.

———. 1969. *The Town Beyond the Wall.* Stephen Becker, trans. New York: Avon.

———. 1970. *Legends of Our Time.* New York: Avon.

INDEX

Aichinger, Ilse: *Herod's Children*, 160-61 n 10
Akhmatova, Anna: "Requiem," 167 n 16
Allende, Isabel: *Eva Luna*, 12, 20, 46, 65-67, 70, 71-73, 74, 76, 80, 83, 85, 98-100, 128-29, 162 n 1, 165 n 12, 166 n 14; *House of the Spirits*, 87, 100-101, 117, 129, 146-47, 157 n 8; *Of Love and Shadows*, 18, 39, 68-70, 92-94, 129, 145-46, 159 n 7, 168 n 20
Anatoli, A. (Kuznetsov): *Babi Yar*, 17, 160-61 n 10, 169-70 n 5
anthropological constant, 137, 149
Appelfeld, Aharon, 114; *The Age of Wonders*, 131-35, 173 n 16; *Badenheim 1939*, 106-10, 129, 163 n 4, 168 n 1; *For Every Sin*, 168 n 1; *The Immortal Bartfuss*, 113, 124-28, 170 n 9, 172-73 n 15; *The Retreat*, 106-8; *To the Land of the Cattails*, 82-83, 103, 168 n 1; *Tzili: The Story of a Life*, 37-38, 82, 106, 134, 156 n 4, 164 n 9, 168 n 1, 168-69 n 2, 170 n 8, 171 n 10, 174 n 4
Arendt, Hannah, 7
Asturias, Miguel Angel: *Mulata*, 21, 22, 36, 51-52, 77, 79, 127

Babel, Isaac: *Red Cavalry Tales*, 28; "Prishchepa's Vengeance," 28-30

Bachelard, Gaston, 137
Bakhtin, Mikhail (M.M.), 2, 24, 25, 31, 76, 104, 105, 115, 133, 135, 143, 147, 151, 153, 158 n 3, 159 n 4; "Art and Answerability," 141; concerning Shakespeare, 143-44; Great Time, concept of, 148-49; Menippean satire, 94, 157 n 8; *Problems of Dostoevsky's Poetics*, 1, 4, 6, 12, 22, 104-5, 157 n 8; *Rabelais and His World*, 3, 17, 20, 23, 30, 31, 33-42, 53-54, 103, 119, 127, 128, 130, 142, 150, 169 n 4, 172 n 14; *Speech Genres and Other Late Essays*, 144, 148-49
Begley, Louis: *Wartime Lies*, 33, 58-59, 81, 156-57 n 7, 160 n 10, 167-68 n 19
Bosch, Hieronymus, 22

carnivalesque-grotesque, 31, 33, 115, 138, 142, 152, 153
Carpentier, Alejo: *The Chase*, 96-98, 167 n 18; *Concierto Barroco*, 55, 70-71, 155-56 n 2, 163 n 4; *The Kingdom of This World*, 155-56 n 2; *The Lost Steps*, 54, 67-68, 72, 75, 78-79, 83, 84, 85-87, 89-90, 108, 129, 130, 138, 145, 148, 162 n 1, 164 n 10, 165 n 12, 167 n 18, 172 n 15
Cavani, Liliana: *The Night Porter*, 170 n 7

Clark, Katerina, and Michael
Holquist: *Mikhail Bakhtin*, 174 n
3

Day of the Dead, 157 n 8
de Sade, Marquis, 18
Desai, Anita: *Baumgartner's
Bombay*, 59-60, 62-63
Devil, the, 43
Dostoevsky, F.M., 104; *Crime and
Punishment*, 15; *The Idiot*, 6; Ivan
Karamazov, 113

El Dorado, 72, 162 n 2

Frazer, Sir James: *The Golden Bough*,
3
Fuentes, Carlos: *The Campaign*,
13-16, 21, 53, 72, 88-89, 91, 117,
127, 143, 162 n 2, 171 n 12,
172-73 n 15
Fuks, Ladislav: *Mr. Theodore
Mundstock*, 52, 105-6, 170-71 n 9

García Márquez, Gabriel, 16; *Autumn
of the Patriarch*, 42-50, 159 nn 5,
6, 163 n 5; *Chronicle of a Death
Foretold*, 94-95, 96; *In Evil Hour*,
21, 51, 55, 65, 74, 91, 158-59 n 3,
165-66 n 13, 168 n 1; "Nobel
Lecture," 156 n 3; *One Hundred
Years of Solitude*, 7-9, 33, 51, 62,
117, 146, 158 n 2, 163 n 5,
166-67 n 15
Gogol, Nikolai/Gogolian, 89, 103-4,
148, 156 n 6; *Dead Souls*, 104
Greenaway, Peter: *The Cook, The
Thief, His Wife, and Her Lover*,
173 n 1
grotesque realism, 41, 91, 100,
103-35, 138, 139-40, 147

Holocaust, literature of, 5-7, 9, 10,
34, 36, 40, 41, 81, 93, 95, 99, 100,

101, 105, 121, 124, 125, 126, 131,
132, 139, 172 n 14
Hugo, Victor, 35

Ivanov, Viacheslav (V.V.), 55, 87,
147

Jakobson, Roman, 150
Janus face, 10, 12, 16, 99, 100, 101,
119, 138, 156 n 6
Jung, Carl, 105, 148; archetype/
archetypal, 2, 4, 11, 31, 64, 108,
111, 149-53, 173-74 n 2, 174 nn
5, 6; collective unconscious, 79,
149, 150, 152; critique of
Nietzsche, 140-41

Kaniuk, Yoram: *Adam Resurrected*,
12, 13, 35, 37, 38, 39, 56-58, 83,
114-15, 158 nn 1, 2, 164 n 7,
172-73 n 15
Koestler, Arthur: *Arrival and
Departure*, 6, 169 n 3
Kosinski, Jerzy: *The Painted Bird*, 6,
35, 110-23, 124, 126, 170 n 6

Lachmann, Renate, 17, 37
Leach, Edmund, 74, 144, 147, 162 n
3
Levy, Primo: *The Drowned and the
Saved*, 160 n 9
Lotman, Yury, 147
Lowry, Malcolm: *Under the Volcano*,
157 n 8

Machiavelli, 43
magical realism/realist, 5, 7, 9, 10,
12, 40, 41, 42, 43, 65-101, 116,
118, 119, 120, 124, 127, 128,
131, 137, 138, 139, 140, 144,
145, 146
Malinowski, Bronislaw, 77
Mukarovsky, Jan, 137
myth, concepts of, 77-78, 81, 163-64

Index

Neher, André: *The Exile of the Word*, 61, 170 n 8, 172 nn 13, 14
Nietzsche, Friedrich, 12; Appolonian-Dionysian antinomy, 138-141, 156 n 6; *The Birth of Tragedy*, 11

Odyssey, The, 132, 157-58 n 9
official vs. unofficial culture, 20, 24, 25, 30, 142-43, 151, 157-58 n 9

Pasternak, Boris: *Doctor Zhivago*, 172 n 15
Patterson, David: *The Shriek of Silence*, 36, 38
Picard, Max: *The World of Silence*, 162 n 12, 171-72 n 12

Rabelais/Rabelaisian, 17, 23, 30, 33, 37, 45, 128, 173 n 1; *Gargantua and Pantagruel*, 23
Rabon, Israel: *The Street*, 17, 55-57
Rector, Monica, 169 n 3
Red Army, 99, 122
Renaissance, 6, 143, 157 n 8
Renaissance grotesque, 35-36, 39
Romantic grotesque, 35-36, 39, 40, 41, 169 n 4
Rulfo, Juan: *Pedro Paramo*, 19, 25-28, 90-91, 117, 157 n 8, 157-58 n 9
Russian Civil War, 17, 28

Sabato, Ernesto: *The Tunnel*, 148
Santayana, George, 41
Second World War, 5, 6, 17, 40, 94, 105, 111, 124

self and other, concept of, 24, 27, 76, 133
Solzhenitsyn, Alexander: *Cancer Ward*, 16; and Gulag Archipelago, 16
Stalin, Josef, 43, 159 n 5

Terras, Victor, 4
Thomas, D.M.: *The White Hotel*, 17, 107, 121, 160-61 n 10
time, representations in narrative, 73-75, 84-86, 106, 144-49, 162-63
Tynjanov, Jurij, 6, 150

Vargas Llosa, Mario: *Conversation in the Cathedral*, 21, 89, 162 n 1, 165 n 13, 171 n 11; *In Praise of the Stepmother*, 103; *The Real Life of Alejandro Mayta*, 59, 68, 87-88, 161-62 n 11; *The Storyteller*, 75, 77-84, 86, 103, 127, 130-31, 145, 163 n 6, 164 n 8, 164-65 n 11; *The War of the End of the World*, 21, 123, 156 n 5, 165 n 13, 166-67 n 15, 167 n 17

Wiesel, Eli, 114; *The Gates of the Forest*, 36-37, 38, 39, 61, 62, 108, 127, 146; *Legends of Our Time*, 172 n 14; *The Town Beyond the Wall*, 38, 52, 60-62, 113, 132-33, 158 n 2, 160 n 8, 169 n 4
Word, the, concepts of, 125-30, 171 n 12

www.ingramcontent.com/pod-product-compliance
Lightning Source LLC
Chambersburg PA
CBHW032045150426
43194CB00006B/430